*Aristotle's Vision of Nature*

# ARISTOTLE'S VISION
# OF NATURE

FREDERICK J. E. WOODBRIDGE

*Edited with an Introduction by*

JOHN HERMAN RANDALL, JR.

*with the assistance of*

*Charles H. Kahn and Harold A. Larrabee*

GREENWOOD PRESS, PUBLISHERS
WESTPORT, CONNECTICUT

Library of Congress Cataloging in Publication Data

Woodbridge, Frederick James Eugene, 1867-1940.
    Aristotle's vision of nature.

    Reprint. Originally published: New York : Columbia
University Press, 1965.
    1. Aristotle.   I. Randall, John Herman, 1899-
II. Title.
[B485.W6   1983]              185               83-12756
ISBN 0-313-24131-7 (lib. bdg.)

Reprinted with the permission of Columbia University Press

Reprinted in 1983 by Greenwood Press
A division of Congressional Information Service, Inc.
88 Post Road West, Westport, Connecticut 06881

Printed in the United States of America

10 9 8 7 6 5 4 3 2 1

For

Helena Woodbridge Wolfe

The Trustees of Union College, Schenectady, New York, have generously provided funds toward the cost of publication of this work, incorporating the Ichabod Spencer Lectures delivered at Union College, November, 1930.

# *Preface*

During Professor Woodbridge's career as teacher and dean of the graduate faculties at Columbia University, it was naturally difficult for him to find time to lecture at other institutions. Upon his retirement as dean in 1929, however, and the publication of his book on Plato, *The Son of Apollo,* the same year, it occurred to the members of the Department of Philosophy at Union College, Schenectady, that he might be preparing a similar book about Aristotle, which he might be willing to "try out" in the form of public lectures. Professors Harold A. Larrabee and Philip Stanley extended the invitation to Dean Woodbridge in January, 1930, for four lectures in the Ichabod Spencer series to be given in November, 1930, and it was accepted.

The lectures on "The Philosophy of Aristotle" were delivered in the Old Chapel, Union College, on Friday and Saturday, November 7 and 8, and on Friday and Saturday, November 21 and 22, 1930.

The Ichabod Spencer lecture series was established in 1909 by a gift of $25,000 from Mrs. Katherine Spencer Leavitt in memory of her father, the Reverend Doctor Ichabod Spencer of the Class of 1822, long a Presbyterian minister in Brooklyn, New York, and one of the founders of the Union Theological Seminary. The lectures were first limited to psychology, the initial series being given by James Rowland Angell, followed by Hugo Münsterberg, John Dewey, Edward L. Thorndike, and Wolfgang Köhler among others. Later their scope was extended to include philosophy, with lectures by George Herbert Palmer, Charles M. Bakewell, Henry Rutgers Marshall, Hans Driesch, R. F. Alfred Hoernlé, and William Ernest Hocking.

In preparing these lectures for publication, certain of Woodbridge's former students enjoyed the privilege of contributing advice and labor: James Gutmann, Albert Hofstadter, Sterling P. Lamprecht, Edith Taber Lamprecht, Harold A. Larrabee, and John Herman Randall, Jr. Of younger Aristotelian scholars, James J. Walsh lent his careful judgment, and Charles H. Kahn, besides furnishing certain notes indicated by his initials, gave invaluable aid in deciding what parts of Woodbridge's preliminary studies to print in the appendices.

In including Woodbridge's preliminary reflections for his finished lectures, the editors recognize that they are only rough drafts, and would have been completely reworked if he had ever considered publishing them.

This volume is dedicated as Woodbridge himself would have wished.

J. H. R., Jr.

H. A. L.

ἀλλ' οὐ πρῶτον τὸ πνευματικὸν ἀλλὰ τὸ ψυχικόν, ἔπειτα τὸ πνευματικόν.

Howbeit that is not first which is spiritual, but that which is natural; and afterward that which is spiritual.

I Cor. 15.46

ἡ γὰρ νοῦ ἐνέργεια ζωή.

For the exercise of reason is also life.

*Metaphysics,* Book Λ

## FREDERICK J. E. WOODBRIDGE
## TO UNION COLLEGE, NOVEMBER 3, 1930

In response to a request for information as to his topics Mr. Woodbridge wrote:

"You have asked of me something with which I can not comply as fully as I should wish. If I were not now engaged in an intensive study of Aristotle, my lectures, I think, would have been already completed. As it is, I am keeping them somewhat in a fluid state because of the fresh revival of interest in studying him. However, I may tell you that the titles of the four lectures will be as follows:

1. Preliminaries, with a Note on the Logic
2. The History of the Soul
3. Physics and Metaphysics
4. The Life of Reason

"In the first lecture I shall deal with the problem which
Aristotle presents in the history of philosophy as a setting for
my own treatment of him as an interesting man engaged
upon problems of continuing human interest. I want to present Aristotle as a philosopher at work rather than to present
him in his own time or in the history of thought. I shall
close the lecture with a comment on the Logic indicating its
place and bearing on the Aristotelian system. I shall deal especially with Aristotle's consciousness of language and his conception of it as the medium in which what existence is finds
its ultimate expression.

"In the second lecture I shall deal with Aristotle's psychology. My aim will be to show that by making the soul
itself a part of the processes of nature he not only freed himself from many of the perplexing problems of psychology,
but also was led to the consideration of nature at large. With
him nature and soul cannot be divorced. Any attempt to
divorce them ends at last in confusion and makes both
physics and psychology unintelligible.

"In the third lecture I shall deal with Aristotle's theory of
nature and point out that his physics and his metaphysics
are not disassociated branches of knowledge, but part of one
general undertaking. His theory of nature becomes with him
a theory of motion and he finds that motion is at last to be
understood, not in terms of the transference of motion from
one body to another, but in terms of the productive and
living processes of nature. With him, the fact that one moving body may move another is relatively unimportant when
compared with the fact that genetic processes issue in results

which are so different from their origin. This view of motion carries him at last to a theology which is rather unique in the history of thought.

"In the fourth lecture, I shall deal with Aristotle's Ethics and set forth his conception of the good life. I expect also to touch upon his theory of art and poetry. In both instances I shall try to indicate how his whole conception of human life is bound up with his theory of nature. In conclusion I shall try to present Aristotle as a man who by following the subject-matter into which he inquires whither it leads him, ends with a system which lays emphasis on the intelligibility of nature as the moving force of its operations and of our own understanding of it."

Woodbridge's own statement in this letter of his intentions in his lectures makes clear what he conceived himself to be doing in them.

# Contents

# *Introduction*

Frederick J. E. Woodbridge devoted a large part of his scholarly endeavor to the study of Aristotle, from his stay in Berlin in 1890 to the last decade of his life, from which the present volume springs. He wrote nothing on Aristotle himself, but the lectures in his course on Greek philosophy were a delight, and as long as he could find students who had the Greek, he gave yearly seminars on the major Aristotelian writings. He raised up a band of devoted students whom he taught to love and to understand Aristotle as he himself loved and understood him. Many of them have written on Aristotle. Among such must be named Edith Henry Johnson, Abraham Edel, Richard McKeon, Richard Hope, Harold D. Hantz, William Barrett, Clarence Shute, and Emerson Buchanan.

In 1930 Woodbridge was asked to give four lectures on the philosophy of Aristotle at Union College, Schenectady. He did not publish them himself, although he prepared them in finished form. On his death in 1940 this manuscript could not be found. After long search, it turned up several years ago in holograph, and thanks to the careful labors of his daughter, Helena Woodbridge Wolfe, was transcribed and made ready for printing. It is thus the only writing in which Woodbridge's approach to Aristotle, and something of his principles of interpretation, are available in print in his own words.

This small volume is offered in the conviction that it is the most important writing on Aristotle's thought since the revolutionary study of Werner Jaeger in 1923. Its importance does not lie, as did the initial impact of Jaeger, in its contribution to the critical study of the Aristotelian texts. Of that branch of learning Woodbridge was also a master, as his textual commentary here printed as appendices make clear. But he preferred, as in his book on Plato, *The Son of Apollo*—and on this occasion was expected—to devote himself rather to Aristotle's philosophical ideas. The importance of Woodbridge's book lies rather in the field of what it has now become clear was the major contribution of Jaeger also. Jaeger's own suggestions as to the temporal development of Aristotle's thought during his long career have given rise to much discussion, and the end is not yet; there is still little that is with certainty assured. But Jaeger's real importance, a generation of study has revealed, is primarily methodological. After his epoch-making labors, one approach to the Aristotelian writings has become impossible, and another is imperative. It is no longer possible to take Aristotle as all of one piece, as an encyclopedia every line of which must be "reconciled" and made consistent with every other. The *corpus* must henceforth be approached as the collected writings of a man who composed them over a career of some forty years, on different occasions and with varying interests uppermost, a man concerned more to refine and extend his knowledge than to make all his ideas consistent.

The importance of this present book, as of Woodbridge's study of Aristotle in general, is likewise primarily methodological. It suggests a new approach, a new way of asking questions about his thought and of seeking to answer them. Woodbridge has his own conclusions—his convictions, he would frankly admit—and some of the major ones are here indicated. They are bound to provoke discussion and thought among students of Aristotle's philosophy. Aristotle's central concern is not with "metaphysics" or with logic. It is with nature—that nature of which human life is the clearest illustration. Human life in its distinctive operations—the "soul" of man—is the best introduction to the study of nature at large and all that is therein. And the study of nature—as explored in the *Physics*—forms a common enterprise with what Aristotle called "first philosophy," not a rival inquiry. For it leads to the construing of nature in the same terms as the construing of human life—as exhibiting a tendency toward intelligibility, toward a logical articulation. Logic is not a method of inquiry, but a part of the doctrine of nature: it is the best expression of nature's structures and categories. So Woodbridge writes here of the soul, of the doctrine of nature, of the good life, and of language, which can state what nature and life are, and in poetry reveal what man must be. He treats the *De Anima,* the *Physics,* the *Ethics,* the *Poetics,* and the *Organon.*

Woodbridge reaches these conclusions, which deserve careful consideration by Aristotelian scholars, through attempting to recover Aristotle independently of what his successors have said about him. Keenly aware, as an historian of thought, of the controversies he has provoked, Woodbridge approaches Aristotle as a man at work on subjects which interested him, trying to find out what was his own way of working with his materials. He starts with the kind of problems which engaged Aristotle's attention, and the way he dealt with them, rather than with his conclusions, so bound up with the information then available, as well as with the misinformation. For Woodbridge is convinced that the way a man approaches his answers has everything to do with what those answers are. So Aristotle's procedure is fundamental to his conclusions, and those conclusions are to be understood in terms of his procedure. They are not to be understood by starting with the elaborate scheme of categories in which he tried in the end to express the knowledge at which he finally arrived.

For it is starting with the logic that has given rise to the controversies about Aristotle. If the treatises on logic are read first, as they were during the Middle Ages, everything else in Aristotle then seems more or less twisted into illustrations of them. The logic then becomes a rigid framework which things are compelled to fit, instead of the type of expression which knowledge ought to seek to be well expressed. The logic is the outcome of inquiry, the articulation of nature's structure. It is not a method of inquiry with which subject-matters are to be approached. Not for Aristotle, at least. For in his procedure he always goes directly without preliminary to the subject-matter involved, and follows it whither it leads him. Only after he has been so led does he try to give logical expression to what he has been led to by the subject-matter itself. With him, logic is thus more a study of language than it is a method of inquiry. It considers the best ways of saying what nature is, and how its parts are related to each other. And that saying is ultimately what justifies both human life, and nature's processes as a whole.

So it is not with his categories that Aristotle first approaches nature. He goes directly to the world of things displayed in the great panorama of the visible world. That world is the scene of dynamic processes, processes of "movement" in the broadest sense, like the human life which is their clearest illustration. Just as man's life is a movement from looking at the visible world to saying what and how it is, so the world itself is a movement from what is visible toward what is intelligible. This is Aristotle's "theory," his intellectual vision of nature. And this is Woodbridge's "theory" of Aristotle. This is the problem which unifies for Aristotle all his specific problems, and the way he dealt with it. "Aristotle attempted to construe nature ultimately in wholly dynamic categories, and to draw out the implications of the attempt. The distortion arose through opposition to him, based on the assumption that his problems were the same as those which arise when nature is construed ultimately in terms of mathematical and static categories." That is why it was for Aristotle the most obvious of facts, that things must be able to do what they do before they do it. What he throughout tried to express in the best words he could find is how things with powers exercise those powers—how they proceed from "can work" to "working" to "work done," from δύναμις to ἐνέργεια to ἐντελέχεια.

Only the man familiar with the twenty-three hundred years of commentary on Aristotle will realize to the full how liberating and novel is Woodbridge's approach. In emancipating them from the more restricting features of the Aristotelian tradition, it will force scholars to reconsider Aristotle himself and his own thought afresh. But for the man who is happily unencumbered by the long controversies of the tradition, this will seem a clear and simple book, a book that presents Aristotle as he saw himself, as he set about trying to explore and to get into words a nature in which human life is central. For Aristotle, as Woodbridge sees him, was a naturalist just because he was a humanist, interested not in nature as man writ large, but in man as nature writ clearly and in perfected form. As Santayana says in a passage Woodbridge loved to quote, "For Aristotle, everything ideal has a natural basis, and everything natural an ideal development."

Woodbridge's manuscript contained the four lectures in finished form he had delivered at Union College. It also contained preliminary drafts for the first three, or rather, his preliminary reflections upon the themes they were to explore. Woodbridge was in the habit of beginning writing by setting forth, in relatively sustained fashion, the ideas that occurred to him as he reflected and meditated on the subject-matter he was proposing to treat. He would write these out in paragraphs on long, yellow, lined foolscap sheets. He would do the same in carefully studying a dissertation offered for the doctorate, and the habit may well have had its inception in this practice.

In the present case, the preliminary reflections are over twice as long as the lectures that finally emerged. They naturally contain much fuller analyses, and the treatment of topics that are germane but got squeezed out in the interest of keeping within the time allotted. They also follow much more closely the text of the Aristotelian writings on which he is concentrating, the Περὶ Ψυχῆς and the φυσικά. They are especially suggestive for the student of the Aristotelian documents.

But they are included here for what is primarily a more philosophical reason than their elucidation of the thought of Aristotle. Woodbridge announces his own concern as to exhibit a thinker at work, and to illustrate how he raised and formulated his problems and how he tried to answer them. In these drafts we can observe Woodbridge himself at work, raising his problems and exploring the answers. They illustrate his habit of mind, his methods of inquiry, his philosophical temper. They display the exercise of his powers in their "historical" and genetic development, as he was striving to reach the entelechy of his finished chapters. Their interest is not only personal, it is methodological. The chief value of these lectures, it can be said, is to illustrate the illumination that comes through approaching Aristotle's thought through his own procedure, apart from all his theoretical statements of method and his elaborate scheme of categories and termi-

nology. Woodbridge himself not only describes and analyzes
this Aristotelian procedure; in his sketches for his chapters he
also illustrates it. They are here included, therefore, because
they give so admirable a picture of an Aristotelian mind at
work. They show the raw material to which he was able to
give finished form. They display the art which came naturally
to him, and was indeed, philosophically, a second nature.

John Herman Randall, Jr.

*Columbia University*
*February, 1965*

*Aristotle's Vision of Nature*

# I

## Preliminaries, with a Note on the Logic

These lectures are not planned as a contribution to the critical scholarship of Aristotle or to the history of philosophy. I should be happy in making such a contribution, for like every student who has become familiar with the problems involved, I find them alluring and fascinating. History itself has made them so. In spite of our own very considerable achievements, ancient Greece and ancient Athens can still arouse wonder and admiration in us. The "glory that was Greece" was a very conspicuous glory when judged by any standard we may set. It does not grow less by the study of it. The things that were done in that little piece of land received in the fifth and fourth centuries before Christ an expression which became the schooling of the minds of the Western world, as the peoples of that world came successively into power, and became ambitious in their turn to have glory and be remembered. The debt to Greece has to be acknowledged. We cannot repay it, for our creditors are long dead and the heirs of their body difficult to find. But they still may be said to hold a mortgage on our minds. It has been neither liquidated nor repudiated.

It is an interesting speculation—and I have sometimes fruitlessly indulged in it—to try to conceive what our minds would be like if Greece had never been. And when I say our minds, I do not mean some secret agent by means of which we think. I mean rather our minds as displayed in the products of our thinking. We have a natural and excusable tendency to look upon our habits of thought as if they were freely formed through the exercise of a native intelligence. I find it very difficult to convince students that they are not so formed. They are slow to see that heredity here is just as real and just as potent as in biology, even if one cannot see its carriers under a microscope. Its carriers are categories. We use a Greek word to name them, and spend much time in trying to define them with exactness. There is, for example, the category "cause." We employ it constantly. It seems to many of us difficult, if not impossible, to think adequately without it. We agree with Vergil,[1] whom we are this year celebrating,

[1] Vergil was born in 70 B.C., so that 1930 was the two thousandth anniversary of his birth. In that year there was erected in Brindisi, where he died on his return from Greece, a marble tablet with the inscription:

> Qui
> ai termini della Via Appia
>   Publio Virgilio Marone
> il supremo cantore dei campi
>   e dell' impero
> or due milleni di ritorno
>   dall' Ellade

that he is happy who knows the causes of things. Yet when we go to our libraries we can find hundreds of books and articles which try to make clear to us what a cause is. It is a very troublesome category. We try to distinguish it from other categories, such as "condition," "ground," "antecedent," "reason," "force," "agent," "means," "end," and others as well. I have read in John Stuart Mill that the real cause of any event is the whole state of the universe prior to that event. This seems to me to make the category quite useless. And I have heard it suggested that modern science has proved that the category of cause is not a category at all, and that there is no such thing as a cause. That sometimes pleases me, but it leaves me perplexed regarding precisely what it is that has been abolished, and what a cause would be if there were one.

I venture another illustration, the category "chance." With it I have had an experience not altogether happy when I have given courses on metaphysics. But what sense—I cannot resist interjecting the question—what sense is there in saying that an experience which happens is not altogether happy? The question indicates some of the difficulty with the category "chance." It is, however, a very useful category. We employ it constantly. The theory of probability is based on it, and that theory, I have been told, is now one of the most important instruments in scientific investigation. I can be glad to be told

------

l'ultima volta salutò la
   saturnia terra
intorno al suo folgorante lume
adunando gli spiriti immortali
   da lui cantati
a guardia della potenza
   rinnovantesi di Roma

that, because it is interesting to know that what I do do is an integration within limits of what I might do. But my gladness is hurt when I am also told that there can be no such thing as chance, because chance cannot be the cause of an event, and every event has a cause. I know, from sad experience, that accidents or the chances of this mortal life have caused me pain and expense, which have not been at all alleviated by the information that chance can cause nothing at all.

But I should be a little more serious. Perhaps, however, what I have been saying is very serious. It may have much to do with those habits of mind of which I have spoken. It may indicate that these habits are very far from being free from a subtle heredity, which so works in us that we seem to be talking sense on all occasions except on that occasion when we try to make sense out of what we say. Our trouble is in our categories, and our categories are an inheritance and not of our own making. We have inherited them from Greece, and when we find ourselves forced to alter them or invent new ones, it is usually to the Greek language that we go.

So, as I have said, I sometimes idly wonder what would have been the case if we had been free from that inheritance, or had had one of a different sort. My wonder reaches a maximum when I try to imagine ourselves wholly free from distinctions between the theoretical, the experimental, the logical, the moral, the aesthetic, the psychological, the biological, the physical, and the metaphysical. It is not easy. I sometimes suspect that our category "scientific" is an attempt to displace those others. It may be said to be ours, for, although the word is old enough, the use of it as a category is fairly new, so new in fact that it is tempting to say that the reign of "science" has but recently begun, and is not yet as fully recognized as it ought to be. We can use the phrase "scientific knowledge" as if the adjective added a glory to the name, instead of a Latin quality to an English word. If it does add a glory, that glory is by way of contrast to what went before. And this makes the history of what went before at least interesting and at most imperative. For we are still playing with categories and should remember our inheritance. Some understanding of that inheritance seems to be requisite, and a study of its history is one of the best means to that end.

I should be happy in contributing to that history, but the kind of contribution I should like to make I am not prepared to make and I fear I shall never be. I have studied that history enough to become convinced that any new contribution to it, to have much importance, involves information which we do not possess, and certain preliminary studies which have not yet been made. So in these lectures I propose something else than history, but something which I hope is not unrelated to it. What I propose is an attempt to see the kind of problems which engaged Aristotle's attention and the way he dealt with them. I say the way he dealt with them, rather than the way he solved them, because I am not sure how far he solved them, and how far he left them either with no solution or with solutions which are unacceptable. His solutions are delivered to the reader in terms of categories many of which he seems to have invented himself. He is the great source of our own categorical inheritance. During the centuries which intervened between him and us, those categories have had an interesting and perplexing history. That is characteristic of age-old inheritances. We still use much the same terms as he used, or terms derived from his by translation into languages other than his. It is consequently easy to expound him in these terms, but after the exposition is made in this way, there may still be much obscurity regarding what Aristotle's enterprise really was. What was he trying to do? These lectures are addressed to that question.

I shall try to answer this question in certain particulars directly from the Aristotelian writings themselves. There are a number of difficulties in the way of doing this as successfully as one could wish. I am very conscious of them, and of two in particular. There is first the difficulty which arises from the historical and critical questions which the writings present. The history of the writings is obscure. It looks impossible to believe that Aristotle wrote all of them, and it looks possible to believe that he wrote none of them. Between these two extremes it is far from clear what position is most likely sound. That he was, however, responsible for the production of most of them is a fact so well attested that we can be as sure as we can be about anything that happened so long ago, that Aristotle was the author of them, in this sense at least, that they grew out of his energy, his work, and his leadership. They are the products of his genius, even if they are not the products of his pen. So in speaking of them I shall speak without hesitation of him as their author, and speak of his opinions as if I were sure that they were his. But it is clear that if the historical and critical questions were settled, one could be much surer of one's ground.

This difficulty is complicated by the fact that we are not yet sure of the character and purpose of the writings. We are not sure to what audience they were addressed. They do not have the appearance of writings intended, as we should say, for publication. Tradition credits Aristotle with superb literary mastery of the Greek language, but the writings do not support this reputation, except incidentally. There are passages of beautiful precision and expression which go readily into a translation of them, as for example, this from the *Politics:* "Man alone has the sense of good and evil, just and unjust; and it is fellowship in these things which makes a household or a city. . . . He who cannot share or because of self-sufficiency has no need, is no part of a city, but is either beast or god." Sentences with that flavor one would like to write. But the language of Aristotle's books is usually more algebraic than literary. "As perception is to the perceived, so is thought to the thought of," he says, for example, in his *Psychology.* He tortures the Greek language. He coins new words. He twists old ones to suit his purposes. He puts a preposition and an indefinite pronoun together and treats the combination as a noun which we translate "relation." He turns a question into a technical term and asks, "What is the what-is-it of this or that?" And we are tempted to translate that questioning term into "nature" or "form" or "essence." He says that for a thing to be what-it-is is to be a "being," and we under the pressure of history translate that final variation of the verb "to be" into the very perplexing term "substance." But I will not multiply illustrations, and must ask forgiveness for trying to illustrate a passage from Greek to English by the use of English alone. The point, however, is, I hope, clear, that the language of Aristotle is hardly what we call a literary language, and the readers of it could hardly have been a general public.

Obviously, the writings of Aristotle must have been associated in some way with his labors, either as a record of them or as a means of extending them to others. They may be the preserved notes from which he lectured, for he is supposed to have lectured in his school, called the Lyceum. They may be the treasured notes of those who heard him. Either hypothesis is good enough as an hypothesis. But neither is very helpful, for as notes of either speaker or hearer, they too frequently indicate a multiplicity of occasions when the lectures were delivered, or a multiplicity of hearers who attended them. The whole matter looks rather hopeless of solution.[2] There may be no necessity of solving it, but the embarrassment involved is this, there is so much disorder, so many cross references, so many evident misplacements, so many parentheses and omissions, so many elliptical expressions, that the reader readily gets the habit of yielding to mass impressions which are often difficult to support by specific expositions in the text. He must read one book in the light of another. He must make supplementations of his own. He must correct what he reads in one place with one import, by what he reads in another place with a different import. If the writings only went straight ahead progressively and continuously, as they do now and then, they would be far more readable, and there would be far less danger of misinterpretation.

[2] Woodbridge perhaps overstates the hopelessness of the question. There is now general agreement (though not unanimity) among Aristotelian scholars that the extant treatises are Aristotle's *own* notes, probably for use in lecturing. [C. H. K.]

And this brings me to the second difficulty. To go directly to the writings of Aristotle, with historical and critical problems unsolved, increases the danger of misinterpretation. Aristotle had predecessors and followers. He is very conscious of the former, and the latter are very conscious of him. We may place him between the two and see what light they throw upon his own work. So far as his predecessors are concerned, this is far from easy to do, because with the exception of Plato, we know so little about them. Besides this, the little we know about them has in the course of history been so colored by what Aristotle himself said of them, that it is hard indeed not to see them through his eyes. And this is largely true even in the case of Plato. It is the opinion of scholars that we have at our command all that Plato wrote, all, that is, that history has credited him with writing. When, however, we compare this all with what Aristotle has to say of Plato, we find ourselves confronted with one of the most engaging problems of the history of Greek thought. We are forced to conclude that Aristotle had access to more of Plato's works than we are familiar with from the writings of Plato which we possess. Aristotle supports this conclusion. And although Plato gives us hardly a hint that Aristotle ever existed, the traditional life of Aristotle has it that at the age of seventeen Aristotle entered Plato's school, the Academy at Athens, and remained there for twenty years until Plato's death. It is natural, therefore, to suppose that his mind was formed under Plato's teaching, in either agreement or disagreement with the master. The writings of the two men placed side by side present a contrast so antithetical that it has become proverbial to say that all philosophers are either Platonists or Aristotelians. The two men have been antithetical in history, and remain so in most minds today, in spite of frequent efforts to show that the pupil was really the product of the master's teaching.

It does not seem likely, therefore, that one will receive much help by first reconstructing Greek thought prior to Aristotle and then placing him in juxtaposition with it. The reconstruction is altogether too much like projecting Aristotle's comments on his predecessors into the past, and correcting the projection by checking it up with Plato's writings and the writings of his and Aristotle's successors. This is what we usually do. We are, perhaps, not in a position to do anything else. But when I do it myself I become so conscious of the uncertainty of it all, that I am tempted to try something else.

As to Aristotle's successors, the situation is different. Although the history of his writings is very obscure and we cannot say with confidence how many of them were known and accessible century by century, we can carry back the serious study of them with confidence to within three centuries of his own day, and, perhaps closer still. That he was studied and his work continued during these three centuries is certain, but we cannot follow that study as clearly as we can the later. There is a story that the writings of Aristotle, his whole library in fact, were lost to the world for the greater part of these three centuries; but nobody, I believe, believes that today. The evidence is much too strong that the work of Aristotle lived and continued to enlarge itself century by century in the hands of men of his own or other races, like the Jews and Arabs. There is still in this field of the Aristotelian tradition a rich opportunity for historical study, in spite of all that has been done in it. There are, however, two circumstances which make the study difficult. There are, first, very serious gaps in the tradition, and there is, secondly, a controversy about Aristotle beginning in the Middle Ages and continuing to our own day. The gaps are serious enough, and raise many perplexing problems regarding the knowledge of commentators of the works as a whole and of their relation to one another; but I am inclined to think that the controversy is more serious. It involved, I think, a distortion of Aristotle which we have not yet outgrown.

I suppose I ought to state here what that distortion was. If I should do this now in general terms, I fear the statement would sound more intelligible than it would be. Aristotle, as I understand him, attempted to construe nature ultimately in terms of wholly dynamic categories, and to draw out the implications of this attempt. The distortion arose through opposition to him, based on the assumption that his problems were the same as those which arise when nature is construed ultimately in terms of mathematical and static categories. Aristotle himself seems to have been fully conscious of the distinction here involved, and I may, perhaps, make this matter clearer by a quotation from his *Physics*. I must ask pardon, however, for translating the passage in a very homely fashion. "As has been said, that which acts as mover is in motion, and that which is in its power movable is also that of which there is motionless rest, for motion belongs to the former, and motionless rest to the latter. Now working upon the latter as such is the same thing as moving it; this occurs by contact, so that motion is the movable having motion at last." I have tried to reproduce in English the idiosyncrasies of the Greek, but the gist of the matter is this: When a body at rest is moved by another body this other body is itself in motion and impinges on the body at rest. Motion strictly is not a transfer of movement from one body to another, but the change from rest to movement, or the change of what can happen into an actual happening. This change is brought about by contact of the two bodies, but it is not in terms of this contact that motion is to be analyzed. One may not like this dealing with what "can be" and what "is." One may much prefer to deal solely with what is. If we observe solely what is, all we observe is a body in motion hitting another body at rest. Our problem is then, if we want a problem and stick wholly to what it is, the problem of finding some way of measuring the motion of the two bodies, and finding the relation of these measured motions to each other. We pay no attention to the obvious fact that in order to move, a body must first be able to move, or be able to be moved. We take it for granted. Aristotle took it seriously. He was worried about it. He was a little contemptuous of those who in his day and before were content to view nature in terms of the movements and collisions of bodies. He would view nature in terms of its dynamic character, in terms of its power to produce, in terms of what to him was the most obvious of facts, namely, that things must be able to do what they do before they do it.

Now the controversy about Aristotle did much to obscure his main purpose. He was appealed to by some to confute what others were doing and doing in a perfectly legitimate way. These others, for their part, came to look upon him with decreasing respect and sometimes with ridicule. Direct study of him gave place to disputes about him. There can be no doubt that his writings supported the dispute.

When, therefore, we look at Aristotle from the point of view of subsequent history, a good deal depends on where we take our stand. Taking our stand as of today and looking backward, we see the accommodation of him to successive efforts to understand him, either for the profit to be derived from that effort or for use for purposes of controversy or authority. There were times when he was studied for the love of it as with Simplicius. There were times when even the supreme authority was clear. Dante called him the master of them that know. There were times when he was ridiculed, as when Francis Bacon dismissed him with a wave of the hand. What are we to make of it all? The question ought to be changed if we are to be at all enlightened. How do we or should we go to work as a preliminary to making something out of it all? The answer is simple. We put the writings of Aristotle side by side with those of his successors and check up the latter by the former.

Our success in doing this, or, perhaps I ought to say, our confidence of success in doing this, depends upon our confidence in having first successfully found out what Aristotle himself thought and said. We must so far as we can recover Aristotle independently of what his successors have said about him. An attempt of this kind is what I propose. The difficulty in carrying it out is obvious. It is obviously impossible to read Aristotle today as if he had never been read before. One

cannot escape the imminent danger of misinterpretation. As
for myself, I lay myself open to the charge of reading into
his writings what is not there and making him say and think
what he never said or thought. In defense or by way of excuse, I may say two things.

If I read into Aristotle what is not there, I must blame the
writings rather than myself. This is not a good defense, and
it may be a poor excuse. Yet it has a point. I am very conscious that what I have to say about Aristotle has been forced
upon me by a study of him and not by a study of his commentators. I have often gone to his writings for confirmation
of views attributed to him, to find no confirmation of them,
or to find the views altered. For example: I find Windelband
saying that Aristotle introduced logic as "a universal theory
of scientific method preliminary to single practical investiga-
tions." [3] Going to Aristotle for confirmation of this, I find
that what Windelband says is either not true or requires very
considerable alteration. If a scientific method is a method of
inquiry or investigation, I do not find Aristotle using his
logic as such a method. When he inquires, he does so in a
very simple and uncomplicated fashion. Sometimes I think
he is almost incredibly naive. He observes, experiments, and
then states as best he can the results he has found, just like
the most ordinary of men. "What is place?" Aristotle asks,
and begins to answer by saying that the question presents
many difficulties. "The existence of place is held to be obvious
from the fact of mutual replacement. Where water now is,

[3] W. Windelband, *A History of Ancient Philosophy* (New York,
1892), p. 249.

there in turn, when the water has gone out as from a vessel, air is present. When, therefore, another body occupies the same place, the place is thought to be different from all the bodies which were to be in it and replace one another. What now contains air formerly contained water, so that clearly the place or space into which and out of which they passed was something different from both. These considerations then would lead us to suppose that place is distinct from bodies and that any sensible body is in place." (*Physics,* Book IV) Yes, so we may suppose; but he goes on in the same manner to bring home a quite different conclusion, namely, that to talk about such a place is to talk about nothing at all, or at best about something about which nothing can be said that has meaning. This is quite typical of Aristotle as an inquirer or investigator. He goes directly without preliminary to the subject-matter involved and follows where it leads him. We are prone to ask a host of preliminary questions before starting to inquire, questions of a logical and epistemological character, but these do not seem to trouble him as preliminaries. They trouble him only in the end.

But his logic may be a theory of scientific method, if it is not taken as a preliminary to inquiry. If we take a theory of scientific method to mean an exhibition of the ultimate form which the expression of the results of inquiry ought to take, then the Aristotelian logic may be said to be just that or something like it. Science, Aristotle thought, ought ultimately to be stated in a way that would make clear the relation of separate statements to one another. It should be as systematic as possible. Now system is introduced into science through the operation of language. Science is, as a matter of fact, just what things or the world are said to be. In saying what things are, we find coherences in what is said. The study of the coherence is logic. And this study is decidedly worth while, because we esteem a science excellent and satisfactory just in proportion as it approaches coherent expression. Logic with Aristotle is thus more a study of language than it is a method of inquiry. This view of the matter has been forced upon me by the study of him. It was not a view I expected to find from that study. From what I had read about him I expected to find something different.

I could give other illustrations of the same kind, to indicate my egotism in supposing that what I read into Aristotle is read out of him. There is, however, a circumstance about the writings of Aristotle, which, I think, makes an attempted independent reading of them more promising than it would be without this circumstance. The writings reveal to an attentive reader of them Aristotle's own way of working with his materials. If attention is fixed on this way of working first, before attention is fixed on result, many difficulties are cleared up. For example, in his treatise *On the Soul* there is in the first chapter a number of questions well calculated to excite the reader's curiosity about the answers which will be given. He asks what the soul is, under what category it should be put, whether it is a potentiality or actuality, whether it has parts or no parts, whether we should consider it or its functions, whether it is exclusively human, whether it is divided or not, whether it is separate from the body or not, and other questions besides. Most of the questions are answered in one way or another somewhere in the book, but the *approach* to these answers has everything to do with what these answers are. Divorced from that approach they are sometimes meaningless and sometimes absurd. Now the approach can be worked out, and when this is done, the questions are then seen to be questions the answer to which depends on the approach to them, in such a way that the answer might well be different from a different approach. I shall try to make this clearer when I examine the psychology later. The thing I want to emphasize here is that Aristotle's procedure is fundamental to his conclusions, so that his conclusions are to be understood in terms of his procedure. It is too often the conclusions which engross the reader, and the procedure is forgotten. The latter can, however, be worked out without considering the independent validity of the conclusions. In trying to work it out, I think one gains a better idea of what Aristotle was trying to do than one gets by asking for the contribution he made to the history of thought. In other words, I think that Aristotle can be studied simply as a sample of a man at work on subjects which interested him. He admirably records the way he works. His conclusions may be nonsensical, but I find it interesting to discover how a man comes to conclusions, nonsensical or otherwise. And I think that an effort of this kind is a preliminary to a consideration of a man's place in history. These lectures then will be, as I have said, an attempt to see the kind of problems which engaged Aristotle's attention and the way he dealt with them. They will not be concerned with what we call his contribution to knowledge, nor with the validity of his conclusions.

I must, however, confess to some enthusiasm about him, and admit that this enthusiasm may sometimes carry me beyond the limits I have set.

Although this lecture has been engaged almost exclusively with preliminaries, I hope it has served also as an introduction to Aristotle. I would now make the introduction a little more intimate by returning to the Logic. The sentence I quoted from Windelband has a significance which I did not recognize at the time. The Logic of Aristotle is, if I may say so, spattered over everything he wrote. If his treatises on logic are read first, everything else seems to be more or less twisted into illustrations of them. This may be what Windelband means by saying that the Logic is a theory of scientific method preliminary to specific inquiries. Now this insistence on logic, or, perhaps, I should say this insistence *of* logic, its continual intrusion into the subject-matter, no matter how varied this subject-matter may be, is something which is provocative. It deserves attention among the preliminaries, and may deserve attention again at the end.

In the first place, a word about the word "logic" itself. I have taught logic, and the first lesson has usually been devoted to a consideration of what logic is. The definition which still haunts me is that given by Jevons in his *Lessons,*[4] namely, "Logic is the science of the necessary and formal laws of thought." This was followed by a consideration of science, and the question was raised whether logic was a science or an art, with emphasis on science and a leaning toward art. Then there was a consideration of "necessary," "formal," "law,"

---

[4] W. S. Jevons, *Elementary Lessons in Logic* (Macmillan, 1905), p. 1.

and "thought." I doubt whether this would ever have happened if Aristotle had never been. At any rate, he is largely responsible for it, and responsible also for that recurring conviction or superstition that to be logical is not only desirable, but it is also to be in possession of the key to all existence. "Logic" and the "Logos" are words to charm with. It is very doubtful if they were such with Aristotle, even if we are forced to say that he solved the final problem in his system by converting what the system logically demanded into the condition on which it depended. Both these words are derived from the Greek word which means "to say," and their derivation is not difficult to follow. Socrates, for example, is said to be a man. But in being said to be a man, he is also said to be mortal. There is a connection between these sayings, a "sayful" or a logical connection. It is the examination of this connection and of what goes with it which gives us the Logic. As for "logos," it is anything that is said, from a word to a book. It is a saying, so that anything that is said, or can be said, is so far forth a "logos." The term slips over quite naturally to something a little different, as may be recognized in one of its Latin equivalents, *ratio* and our own "ratio" and "reason." For example, if John is said to be the brother of James, or 4 is said to be twice 2, or fire is said to be where there is smoke, there is in each of these cases and in cases like them something which is called a "logos," in consequence of which these several sayings are said, and said in their particular ways. So also if Socrates is said to be a man, there is a "logos" which is relevant to saying so. The "logoi" which are thus relevant to whatever is said become matters of logical interest. Aristotle often calls them "categories," a word which to the Greek ear usually meant "accusation," for "to categorize" was to accuse some one of something. The accusation was a category. So when John is said to be the brother of James, there is a category on which that accusation is founded. In the treatise on the categories, ten of special significance are named; but in the writings as a whole there are evidently many more than ten.[5] Neither the number nor their names is just now important. The important thing is that Aristotle is quite convinced that our knowledge is in the best shape when the logical connections in it are clear, and everything that is said is said relevant to a system of categories. This is why, as I have said, the logic, although it has special treatises devoted to it, intrudes itself generally throughout the writings. This is why so many of the treatises begin with questions regarding the appropriate categories for the subject-matter in hand. And this, I may add, is why, centuries later, the logic of Aristotle became a rigid framework which things were compelled to fit, instead of the type of expression which knowledge ought to seek to be well expressed.

But I cannot even now let the logic go with this disposition of it. The more I study it and observe its ever-present character, I come to have a vivid impression of Aristotle's own consciousness of language. I should find it difficult to substantiate by direct reference to his works, even to my own satisfaction, what I am now about to say. In some respects it might better be said at the end. But I have become so im-

[5] When Aristotle enumerates the categories in other writings, he lists fewer than ten. Woodbridge is apparently using "category" in the broader sense developed at the beginning of this chapter. [C. H. K.]

pressed by this consciousness of language that I think something ought to be said here about it, even if other things might well be said first.

It is obvious enough, although rarely taken seriously, that language is not only the expression of what we know, but is also the actual physical embodiment of knowledge. It is knowledge in physical shape. We often use the expressions, "the body of knowledge," and "the body of truth," but "body" here can be something besides a metaphor. Language is a body and operates as a body. It is a cause of effects. It brings into being what would never be brought into being without it. It operates. Otherwise we should not be here tonight, with the hazardous expectation that an hour or so of language will illuminate a figure out of the distant past, that a bombardment by words connected in a certain way will change the things bombarded by them. This sort of operation is happening nearly every hour of the waking day. It happens, or something like it, even in our hours of meditation, for we have the best of evidence for an internal language which is actual physical disturbance. It can be felt. It can wear one out and make one tired. It can, to a degree, be measured. Yet in spite of all this, we have quite generally the habit of supposing that language is not a working body along with other working bodies, a force along with other forces, just as much a factor in nature's domain as any other. We are prone to regard it as a kind of persiflage curiously playing over the surface of things, sometimes making sense and sometimes nonsense. We accuse men of verbalism, categorizing this language unfavorably. Now, as I read Aristotle, this is something which he does not do. He takes language seriously, and he takes it as a natural or physical event. He sees in it well-nigh the most important event in the world. He is impressed by the human effort to get things properly said, and by the fact that just in proportion as this is done, man finds himself in possession of an instrument by means of which he directs the forces at his command. He is impressed by something so obvious that when once it is pointed out everybody has a tendency to say "naturally" or "of course." But he will not let the naturalness of language be natural in admission only. He makes it natural in nature. It becomes one of nature's supreme products, the product in which all other products find articulated linkage. For things to go into language is as a going, just as much of a going on their part, and just as natural, as their going into air or water, up or down, or from seed to flower. It is a going which requires for its elucidation precisely the same sort of factors that are required for any other sort of going. And it is the only sort of going which makes sense out of existence. Socrates *is* a man. He is *said* to be a man, and only when he is said to be such, is he in any sense intelligible, because it is only language which can declare what Socrates is.

When the Logic of Aristotle is read in this fashion, it becomes a part of his physics, or better perhaps, a part of his entire doctrine of nature. That he should be so much influenced in his categories by the parts of speech is not surprising. That he should find in the moods and tenses of verbs something more significant than he finds in nouns and adjectives is natural. He is very fond of the Greek idiom which combines the neuter definite article with the infinitive mood of the verb, which helps to put an emphasis on action and process. He begins the *Metaphysics* with a sentence "πάντες ἄνθρωποι τοῦ εἰδέναι ὀρέγονται φύσει." We translate "All men naturally have a desire of knowledge." But the τοῦ εἰδέναι is a little baffling when we try to get its entire flavor into English. "Knowing" may do it if we stress the second syllable, and so make it clear that we have an infinitive and not a participle. Then we can see that it is the bringing of one's knowing process to function that is desired, and that man is marked by something more than curiosity. Since language is thus a natural product, the logic of language tends to exhibit the categories in terms of which nature operates. Because Socrates is a man, he is mortal. Aristotle was not so silly as to suppose that a syllogism could kill a man. But he was convinced that without the logic of that syllogism not even the Athenians could have put Socrates to death. Aristotle was a man very fond of words, but I must believe that he was fond of them because of a consciousness of their natural power, and because he believed that if there is any system of things, that system must be of a kind that permits the factors which make it a system to get over into the language of men. The system must somehow be what it is said to be. If we are able to say what things are, what they are must be something that can be said, and in getting said they have reached, perhaps, the end of their career.

# II

## The History of the Soul

"Since we rate knowledge among the fair and valued things, and one type higher than another either in precision or in being knowledge of the better and more wonderful, for both these reasons we should rightly put the history of the soul first. Knowledge of it seems to be of great consequence for truth generally and particularly for truth about nature." In this manner Aristotle begins the treatise which is usually cited by its Latin title *De Anima,* and which we call his *Psychology.* His own expression, the "history of the soul," is more attractive, although history did not mean for him precisely what it means for us. With the Greeks generally, as is illustrated by Herodotus, it usually meant a collection of information about men and cities with some suggestion that the collection was made with care. It could mean also a collection of information about other things, as is illustrated by Aristotle's own *History of Animals.* The word applied to

the soul probably meant with him nothing more. Yet it is
appropriate in our sense. For, according to Aristotle, the soul
has a career. It begins with small things and grows to great
things, and its growth has a continuity which can be examined. The history of the soul is thus a happy expression for
information about the soul.

Aristotle rates this history high. I am not sure that he would
have it studied first of all his works, but I am sure that the
study of it first is one of the best of introductions to the others.
It is quite true, as he says, that it has an important bearing on
all truth and particularly on truth about nature or the history
of things—the truth, that is, as he would have one see it. This
is one reason why I begin with it. Another reason is that it
admirably illustrates Aristotle's method of working and gives
an insight into his type of mind. Although, after the promise
of the opening sentences which I have quoted, he deluges the
reader with a series of questions and a use of terms, both
hard to understand, when he gets down to work, he reveals
a method of working which is easy to follow even it it leads
to difficulties which are not easy fully to comprehend. It reveals the man moving toward the problem which became
the final problem of his system, the problem of the ultimate
motivation of genetic processes.

The first question in the history of the soul is, obviously,
what the soul is. This is, as a type of question, the first question to be asked when anything is to be investigated. But in
any case, as in the case of the soul, that about which the question is asked should first be identified. The identification of
subject-matter is preliminary to any question asked about that

subject-matter. No other preliminary is necessary. To call the subject-matter itself in question in any way that would impair the identification of it, is to ruin inquiry at the start. If you don't know to begin with what you are talking about there is no profit in talking about it. By talking about accessible things to begin with, you may be led to talking about inaccessible things, but something must be accessible first. This is fundamental with Aristotle. He begins as naively as a child who takes up a hammer and asks his father, "What is a hammer?" I sometimes think we should all be happier if we all began in that way. I sometimes find men show greater interest in the question, whether we have souls, than in the question, what is the soul we have? The latter and not the former is Aristotle's question.

Now Aristotle thinks that everybody identified the soul in the same way, namely, either by the observable difference between things that live and things that do not live, or by the clearer and more readily observable difference between a living man and a dead one. This difference the Greek language recognized by the current use of words like those we have borrowed from the Latin—"animate" and "inanimate." Everybody was familiar with the difference, or at least talked as if they were. Socrates alive and Socrates dead gave as clear an exhibition as one could have of the difference between his soul and his body. Alive, he had a soul; dead, he either had none or it had gone away. This is not an illustration from the text of Aristotle, but it fits it to a nicety. I am saving his own most telling illustration for later use.

Since the soul is thus identified, what shall we say it is?

The question gets its point for Aristotle from the fact that he finds that those who have written about the soul, and particularly such men as Empedocles and Democritus, who preceded him, used the soul to explain the powers of perception and motion which men have. Men perceive the world in which they live, and they move about in it as if directed in their movements from within, and the soul is invoked to explain these peculiarities. How does it explain them? Aristotle would find out what the soul is first, before he attempts an explanation. The opinions of others give him the approach to his own definition of the soul. Others have defined the soul in terms of its relation to the body, and he follows their example. This relation is the key to the definition. How then are soul and body related? The answers which have been given he reduces to three principal ones. First, the relation has been conceived after the analogy of the relation of two bodies to each other. The soul is in the body as one body may be in another, and, consequently, the soul has been conceived to be something like air or fire or water or even earth. Since the blood is supposed to be mixed of these elements, the soul has been conceived to be like the blood. Because these elements move one another, and because the blood is abundant in the parts of the body when these parts are especially active, the soul moves the body in similar fashion. And perception is explained by the impact of bodies like or unlike it upon the soul itself. But this will not do. It is all too much like that wooden statue of Aphrodite which Daedalus made active by pouring quicksilver into it. If soul and body are related as two bodies are, then soul and body should be separable as two bodies are. We should be able to get the soul as soul, just as we get air as air or blood as blood. This we cannot do, and so there is no profit in trying to define what the soul is in terms of a relation like the relation of two bodies to each other. The soul is not to the body as water is to fire, nor as blood is to the heart, even if one defines anger as the seething of the blood about the heart. A different sort of relation must be found.

Two other analogies have been suggested, that of harmony and the sounds which produce it, and of number and that which is numbered. The soul is thus defined either as the harmony of the body or the number of it. Aristotle has both respect and disrespect for these definitions. He respects them because they evidently attempt to get away from an exclusively bodily relation. They indicate an effort to conceive the soul as something quite different from quicksilver. He disrespects them, however, because the first is reducible to a bodily relation, and the second is quite unintelligible. Harmony, when analyzed, is found to be a blending of sounds which are themselves distinct; and when these sounds blend, the result is another sound. It is pretty to say that the soul is the harmony of the body, but it will not do. As for saying that it is the number of the body, this is little more than excited nonsense. Numbers are of the greatest importance. They enter into every exact calculation, and make mathematics a powerful instrument in constructing things; but to talk of a moving or perceiving number is to talk nonsense. But the number men seem to talk that way. They make numbers make the world. They are too much like enthusiasts, blinded by the emotional effect of the beauty and value of their own branch of knowledge. They have nothing to contribute to the definition of the soul.

What then is the proper analogy? Aristotle's own answer is the analogy of an ax and its cutting. He goes first to what is inanimate. The soul is related to the body as the cutting of an ax is related to the ax, or, in general, as what a thing does or can do to the thing that does it. We can put this into familiar categories and say, the relation is that of function and structure, but it is better to have a homelier expression in mind at first—the doer and what it does—and see, with Aristotle, the soul as simply the doings of the body. But it seems a little absurd to say that cutting is the soul of an ax. Yet Aristotle reminds us, although withholding his approval, that Thales said that the magnet has a soul because it attracts iron. This is, however, evidence that we give souls to things in consequence of what they do. We give them at least the power to do it, converting the fact that they can do what they do into the category of power. The soul, then, is first of all a power.

Here I must digress in the interest of not being led astray by that powerful category. It is one of Aristotle's best beloved. It is one which has played a powerful role in the history of thought and in the controversy, often bitter, over Aristotle. We do not like the doctrine of powers. They seem to be so inadequate for the explanation of anything. It is common enough to ridicule the imbecile who said that opium puts a man to sleep because it has a dormitive power. Yet I sometimes wonder in moments when I am off my guard whether it could put a man to sleep if it lacked that power. And I find myself, even when I am on my guard, using such words as "is," "may," "might," "can," "could," "would," and "should." I find it quite impossible to get on with "is" alone, except, perhaps, in mathematics, and even there I find it difficult whenever I meet a variable or attempt an integration. Those little words I have enumerated, to which I might add that potent word "if," invoke in me a powerful respect. If three points are in the same plane, a circle *can* be drawn whose circumference contains them. I cannot seem to get on without that "can." My language would be useless without it, as I am just now abundantly proving by its use. I cannot get on without power, for power is at least the power to say "can."

Is all this just nonsense? I will not take the time to try to answer that question. Perhaps I have not the power to answer it. Yet I hope I have made it clear that power is not easy to escape. We buy it and sell it. We want as much of it as we can get. We sometimes stake our lives on getting it, on getting that which enables us to do what can be done. If only I had the power to make this clear, I might rival Aristotle in reputation. But, perhaps, I have made clear how a category arises by indicating that in the use of language "power" becomes a term to cover what a thing can do. Since playing with words is often in some queer way an aid to clearness, I might vary my words and say, what anything is able to do is its ability, and then equate "ability" and "power." In Greek, δύνασθαι is equal to what "to be able" is in English, and δύναμις is equal to "ability." That we use "power" instead of "ability" when we expound Aristotle is clearly not his fault.

Nor is he responsible for the notion that the power of a thing makes the thing do what it does, as if the ability of an ax to cut made it chop wood. This notion he was at considerable pains to set aside. Indeed, he says explicitly that if powers alone were effective, everything that can happen ought already to have happened. So when the soul is called a power, a category ought not to lead us to make an improper accusation. I shall stick by "power" because it becomes increasingly powerful. Its ability grows.

The soul is, then, first of all a power. But the ax with its ability to cut is not a wholly satisfactory example, for the ax is not alive. It does not cut without somebody to use it to cut with. A man, however, does what he does without anybody to use him to do it with. He sees with his own eyes, not with the eyes of another, nor does another use his eyes to see with as he might use a microscope. He operates his own instruments. And it is just this operating of one's own instruments which distinguishes the living from the dead and from the nonliving. Aristotle makes a good deal of this distinction. It is very fundamental with him. Forgetfulness of it makes him quite unintelligible. To follow him we must start with it or not expect to follow at all. It is easy to distinguish the "animate" from the "inanimate" superficially, for the former live, as we say, while the latter do not. But what is it to live? This is a troublesome question, but Aristotle has an answer: to live is to have a start of motion in oneself; not to live is to have a start of motion outside oneself. We can quarrel with this, but we mustn't quarrel with it if we are to get on with Aristotle. And I suspect that quarreling with it might have

no other effect than turning the "inanimate" into the "animate" or the "animate" into the "inanimate," thus leaving us
more distressed over the distinction between the two. So long
as we do not identify them and so drive both the "animate"
and the "inanimate" out of both language (sense) and existence, we need some distinction. Aristotle was unwilling to
identify them, because he thought that the difference in the
start of motion which he defined was so obvious and so observable. He observed it when he looked at a house which was
built by a carpenter and then looked at the carpenter.

The soul as the power of the body must, therefore, find a
better illustration than the ax with its power to cut. Aristotle
invents one. "If the eye," he says, "were an animal, vision
would be its soul." It is an excellent illustration for his purposes and, perhaps, could not be better. For it is the eye that
sees, or if one prefers, a man that sees by means of the eye,
and the seeing is its or his own and not another's. Besides this,
the illustration has done something to the power. For it is
vision now which is the soul of the eye—not the power to see,
but actual seeing. And here we stumble on another of Aristotle's categories, ἐνέργεια, the companion and often the rival
of δύναμις. We get our word "energy" from it, but should
forget that we do when Aristotle is read. For energy with
him is like our "working": it is power exercised, ability in
operation, the start of motion from within started on its way.
In order to have a soul, it is not enough to be able to see,
there must be vision also. And this fact makes vision a problem in the history of the soul. It is the problem of perception.
For the eye sometimes sees and sometimes does not. That it

can see is no more a problem than that the ax can cut, but when it does see there is a problem, just as there is a problem when the ax cuts. Not the power of vision but vision in the working, vision "in energy," is the problem, and there is need of a theory of vision to solve it. I shall deal with this theory later. I mention it here when it is natural to mention it, and because it may now be seen that Aristotle makes the problem of perception a derivation of what the soul is. The problem follows from the definition of the soul. So we must return to the definition.

I will not continue to build up the definition in the manner which I have hitherto followed. It would take too long. Enough has been said, I hope, to show how Aristotle goes to work, to give some idea of the way he builds up his system. We go from identifications to observations about what has been identified. These observations are criticized until the appropriate or promising ones are sifted out and point to some statable result. Then the result is stated in what are called the "categories," which have the effect of tying together what has been said in a manner which implies the whole genetic process by which the result has been reached. This is the method of Aristotle. The "categories" are what the investigation culminates in. They are ends reached, and not beginnings which constrain the inquiry. But this should be added: when the categories become systematized, it becomes natural to begin any fresh inquiry with the question, "What categories are here appropriate?" Aristotle does this so repeatedly that it is, perhaps, natural to suppose that he goes from categories to things and not from things to categories. But his way of working shows quite clearly that the categories are developed out of his procedure in dealing with things.

To return to what the soul is: it is at last defined as "the first entelechy of a natural organic body." This is cryptic enough, but perhaps not so cryptic as it would be without the preliminaries which I have sketched. This final definition is preceded by another which is a little simpler: "the soul is the first entelechy of a natural body having the power of life." About the only trouble here is with that "first entelechy," for the rest of the definition seems clear enough. And it is clear that in the final definition "organic" has simply replaced the longer and more cumbersome expression, "having the power of life," for to have this power is to have organs exercised in consequence of a start of motion from within. All that is now left is that "first entelechy." Instead of "entelechy" our translations often use the word "realization." This fits the Greek fairly well, but since there is no English word as near to the Greek as one desires, his word has simply been translated and has had some currency even in recent biological speculations. Now Aristotle coined the word "entelechy," and I suppose a cultivated Greek of his day had no difficulty in seeing why he coined it. He made it up of three words "in," "end," and "to have." [1] So we may say it meant that which is had or possessed in the end. It is a sort of realization or fulfillment of what has gone before or of operating conditions. It

---

[1] The standard etymology of ἐντελέχεια, referred to here by Woodbridge, which dates from the Renaissance, is linguistically impossible: -έχεια has nothing to do with ἔχειν, to have. The term seems to be an abstract noun derived from the adjective, ἐντελής, "perfected" or "completed." [C. H. K.]

sums up what has been said about the eye having the power to see and about vision as a consequence of the exercise of that power. It means the ability and its exercise and its result all in one. Were the ax alive, its power to cut exercised in actual cutting would be its "entelechy" or soul.

The word "first" has troubled commentators, and it is pretty sure to trouble any reader. It probably means first in the sense of "first time" or "at the moment." "First entelechy" is the very instant of entelechy, just as we may say that it is exactly twelve o'clock when the clock strikes. It goes on striking, but the first stroke is the realization of its power to strike. But, perhaps, "first" is a matter of exactness rather than of importance. The important point is that the soul has now been defined as the body's power exercised. And Aristotle immediately concludes that there is no more sense in asking whether the body and soul are one than there is in asking whether the wax and the impression on it are one.

We may now ask, what does Aristotle gain by this definition? It looks like little more than the condensed expression of an elaborate analysis. That is what it is. But is not that precisely what every decent definition is? And is it not by getting such definitions that one's mental perspective is altered and enlarged? Do not such definitions become in their turn powerful instruments of analysis? Do they not help to organize our knowledge and put it on the way to becoming a system? Aristotle would answer these questions in the implied affirmative. By his definition he freed himself from many of the entanglements of his predecessors. He changed a current attitude toward the soul and its problem. He took the soul out of the realm in which such men as Empedocles and Democritus had put it—and the harmony men and the number men. He took it also out of the realm where those had put it who saw in it something that, keeping its identity, transformed itself through countless years into different forms of life. He made its home in nature, and by so doing was forced, as we shall see, to enlarge the conception of what nature is. He said, it may be recalled, that a knowledge of the history of the soul has much to do with the truth about nature.

One enlargement of perspective may be noted at once. His definition of the soul made the soul coextensive with the whole of life. Everything that lives must have a soul. Man has no exclusive claim upon it. Plants and animals, from the lowest to the highest, have it. The difference between plants and animals on the one hand and man on the other is not that the latter has a soul and the former none. It is a difference only in the kind of soul they have. It is the soul, not life, that makes distinctions among the living. And if we would make the distinctions precise, the hint for doing so lies in that word "organic." He devotes a treatise to the "parts" of animals to bring out his contention that the true parts are organs, instruments of an entelechy, and not like parts of a machine. So a living being has more or less soul just in proportion as it has more or less organs. To say that a plant has a soul is not to say that it sees or thinks, for the only organs discoverable in it are those of nutrition and reproduction. But to say that a man has a seeing and a rational soul is not to free him from the soul of a plant as well, for he too has organs of nutrition and reproduction. So the soul does have a history, and a history inextricably bound up with nature at large. It can be adequately understood only in proportion as nature itself is understood. It cannot be taken out of nature, leaving nature to be construed without it. Or if this is done, then we should remember that what we then have is a science of nature with the naturally living left out, just as in geometry we have a science of surfaces and solids with every surface and every solid left out. Such a science of nature would not give us what nature is, any more than geometry gives us what surfaces and solids are. The definition of the soul is rather a powerful definition. It does seem to have a bearing on the whole of truth.

I must omit Aristotle's exposition of the different kinds of soul and of their relation to each other. It is enough to say that his exposition follows the lines we might expect it to take, the lines, namely, of his observations of the structure and functions of living beings generally. His observations were not always faultless, but what impresses the modern reader is the number that are correct and the wide range they cover. And we do not have a record of them all. The thing that chiefly troubles such a reader is the apparent conviction on Aristotle's part that the forms or species of life are fixed. I say apparent, because I am not sure. Aristotle has the habit of taking things pretty much as he finds them in the shapes with which he was familiar. In this sense species are with him fixed just as they are with us. But his whole system is built up in view of a developing nature. He comes so near to being in some sense an evolutionist that it is hard to tell how far. The idea was not alien to his thought. It had been expressed long before his day. But his interest seems to have been predominantly in something else, in the immediate nature which he observed, described, and tried to express in his system.

So I omit the history of the different kinds of soul, and turn to the two problems the soul presents, the problems of perception and motion. How is it that the soul perceives what it does perceive, and how does it move the body? This is an unfortunate way to state the problems, as Aristotle himself observes, for it is strictly the whole man—and I confine myself here to the human soul—it is the whole man, body and soul, that perceives and moves. How then does a man with a soul perceive and move? He does both. That is not to be forgotten. No explanation is sought for the power he undoubtedly has. With that we start or we cannot start at all. But how is that power exercised? Or we may change the question again and ask, what are perception and motion? how are they to be defined when emphasis is put on the soul?

I wish I were sure of Aristotle's precise answer to this question. He evidently had a good deal of difficulty with it. What he says about it is scattered and not, so far as I know, expressed in one passage with sufficient clearness so that a reader can make it out. Besides this he says things which are contradictory, on the surface at least. But it is quite clear what he will not have. In his theory of perception he will not have it defined in either of two ways. I will illustrate these ways in the case of vision. Empedocles had held that in vision light or something like it goes out from the eye and illuminates the object seen. This Aristotle dismisses with the remark that we ought then to see in the dark. And he calls absurd Plato's

suggestion in the *Timaeus* that the light going out from the eye in the dark is overpowered by the dark. Democritus had held that in vision the object seen produces a reflection in the eye by means of disturbances coming from the object seen to the eye, and this reflection produces vision. Aristotle dismisses this with the observation that other surfaces besides the eye reflect and yet there is no vision. A mirror does not see, and even if we gave it the power to see, it would not see the reflection in it any more than the eye does. These objections to Empedocles and Democritus seem to make it clear that Aristotle will not have perception to be either an operation of the perceiving organ on the object or an operation of the object on the perceiving organ. He will have it something else. It is this something else which I find difficult. I can use Aristotelian jargon and say that perception is the actualization of a perceptible object in a primary perceiving subject. I can quote him to the effect that in perception the soul receives the form of objects independent of their matter. But neither the jargon nor the quotation does for me any more than cover over a difficulty with words. I am unhappy when I try to get away with the matter in this fashion. I must try something else.

Now Aristotle observes that if a membrane of some sort is stretched over the skin, it does not interfere much with touch. We ourselves can observe a man working with rubber gloves on his hands. So we say that the skin is like a natural glove. Indeed, Aristotle insists that in all cases of perception there is a medium of some sort involved. This is one point to be kept in mind. And this point leads directly to another on which he

equally insists, namely, that the natural conditions obtaining
on the occurrence of perception must be the start of any determination of what perception is, for it is objects and not
the soul that we perceive, so that the conditions of perception
are to be sought in the objects and not in the soul. He says
quite explicitly: "In the case of each perception we must
first consider that which is perceived." (*De Anima* II, ch. 6
418a 7)

When this is done, we find that in the case of each perception there is involved the operation on the body of objects of
various sorts through appropriate media, the hard and soft
through the envelope of the skin, the sweet and bitter through
water, odors through air, sounds through air and water, colors
through a transparent medium which we call light. These
are the conditions of perception. I suppose that we could say,
in our manner of speaking, that in every case of perception
there is involved an object, a medium, and a bodily reaction,
and that these constitute the conditions of perception. But
Aristotle says that *what* we perceive is the hard and soft, the
sweet and bitter, and so on. Now it is ridiculous to say that in
perceiving, the soul becomes hard or soft, etc., for these distinctions belong to things and not to the soul. All the soul
does is to become perceptive of them, and it so becomes solely
because it is what it is defined to be, namely, a power. If I
may now use some Aristotelian terms, I would say that perception is the energizing of the soul's power in consequence
of the conditions which are the conditions of perception.

I am afraid that this is not very intelligible. I do not claim
that it is, but I think it does indicate what Aristotle is trying

to do. He is trying to get rid of certain theories of perception which he believes to be wholly unintelligible, and trying to frame a theory more consonant with the facts as he sees them. He rejects the theory that perception is a kind of going out from the body to the thing perceived. This is easy. He rejects also the theory that it is a going into the body from without. This is not so easy, for the examination of the condition under which we perceive forces him to recognize that object–medium–reaction situation. This theory of internal perception, however, does violence to the facts, because in normal perception, what we perceive is not internal to the body, and this is clearly the case with sight. The internal theory makes us see what we do not see at all. And the evidence for this fact, he thinks, is as good as the evidence for any other. If then, we are to have a theory at all, it must be different from those rejected. What then does he do? It seems to me to be something like this. He stands by the conditions of perception, but insists that they are conditions, and nothing more. They are in no sense at all what perception is, and this for the reason that they can all be given and no perception occur. We can blot out the whole visible world simply by closing our eyes, and it is ridiculous to hold that the world is made visible by opening them. How can opening the eyes make colors, when we know by experiment that it is the reflection of light from surfaces that makes them, and that we do not see them in the dark? And if perception is that internal matter, why do we need organs of perception? If the soul can see without eyes—and this is what the internal theory makes it do—why are eyes necessary in order to see a

visible world? I imagine Aristotle asking not just those questions, phrased as I have phrased them, but questions very
much like them. And then I imagine him saying: "Great
Zeus! A man clearly can do what he can do if he has the
chance; he can perceive if he has the opportunity. The conditions of perception give him the chance, and all he does is to
take it. Perception is just like, or a good deal like, building a
house. You must have a carpenter first, a man who can build.
But you must give him the chance to build by supplying him
with some inducement, which comprises the condition under
which houses are built. Then he builds. Democritus, however,
ought to say that he builds the house in his ability to build.
I should say that he actualizes his power to build in a world
of building materials. Why then not say something similar
about perception? For after all my troubles, I come back to
the simple fact that in perceiving things a man simply does
what he can do. Why then construe the situation in such a
manner that he cannot do it?"

Whatever Aristotle's conception of what perception is, it
does two things of particular consequence for his system. In
the first place, it makes the study of perception ultimately an
analysis of what is perceived. It generates theories of the per-
ceivable, all the way from the tactual to the visible. Into these
I cannot go even if his theory of vision is particularly alluring
in view of our own theories of light and color. In the second
place, Aristotle's conception forces him to make the doctrine
of the soul, and in general the doctrine of powers, a doctrine
of nature at large. And he says, the history of the soul has an
important bearing on the truth about nature. In other words,

nature must at least be defined in such a way that the soul is as natural as anything else. And in the third place, Aristotle is forced to set up a kind of correlation between the powers of the soul and the natural conditions of their exercise.

To this last I now turn. I must dismiss with only a remark or two Aristotle's consideration of that motion which man— and other living things—has as a consequence of having a soul. The argument is in its general character the same as the argument in the case of perception. The conditions of motion are analyzed, and when these conditions are given, the power of motion is released. The ultimate power of the soul involved in movement is desire or appetite, and the analysis attempts to show the conditions involved in the operation of desire. I must leave the matter with this summary statement. My main purpose in these lectures is to exhibit Aristotle at work and to illustrate how he raises and solves his problem.

The correlation between the powers of the soul and the natural conditions of their exercise is, perhaps, the one dominant and outstanding characteristic of Aristotle's psychology. In dealing with this correlation in detail he was obviously limited by the knowledge of his day. But the consequences of this limitation have very little to do with the doctrine involved, although they are repeatedly a source of confusion in reading him. It is important, therefore, to get the correlation itself clear. He himself expresses it in one algebraic sentence which may be cited as the key to the psychology (*De Anima* 429a 17): ὥσπερ τὸ αἰσθητικὸν πρὸς τὰ αἰσθητά, οὕτω τὸν νοῦν πρὸς τὰ νοητά. This, I take to mean that for every power of the soul there is an appropriate field of operation in nature.

The powers of the soul are exercised in realms of being congruent with their exercise. This correlation I have tried to illustrate in the case of perception. The soul, for example, has the power of vision, but this power can be exercised only in a field of vision or in a world itself visible, and visible, as it were, in its own right. To put this a little more concretely and perhaps a little more plainly, if we are to see anything, we can see it only in a world which has already been lit up by the action of light. This lighting up of the world is quite independent of the eye and of the soul. It is something that happens in nature, and if it did not happen there, nothing would ever be seen. This illustration, I hope, makes the correlation clear in this instance of it. The correlation is, generally, between two incomparables, between an act and a field of action, and an act and a field of action are as different as can be, but it is only the cooperation of the two that is ever effective. The effect of this correlation in operation is the "conformation" of the soul to what it perceives. It is in the light of this that all the form and matter business is to be interpreted. It is this cooperation of powers with a correlative field that Aristotle tries to work out in detail. This he does, first, by distinguishing powers such as appetite, reproduction, perception, imagination, memory, reason, and secondly, by analyzing the field in which they operate. We may now say that each recognizable power has its correlative field. One power does not grow out of another, as if reason grew out of perception and perception grew out of appetite. There is no evolution of powers, even if the exercise of the higher powers involves, as he maintains, the exercise of the lower. A man is all that an animal is, and an animal is all that a plant is, but the order is not to be reversed, as if the animal grew out of the plant and the man out of the animal. Yet the soul is a unitary power. The exhibition of its activity as distinguishable powers is due to the fact of different fields of action and organs appropriate to them. So there can be an evolution of living beings only on condition that new organs are generated. These are the general outlines within which the psychology moves.

One of the powers of the human soul is reason or thought. Men think and reason as well as perceive and take nourishment. Both are equally natural activities on man's part. But just as the taking of nourishment involves a field of food or food objects, so the exercise of reason involves a field of ideas or ideal objects. In other words, the rational life of man is not something superimposed on his other lives or growing out of them, but is life in a realm of being different from theirs. Nature in its own right must possess such a realm of being, or man could not think at all, just as he could not see at all if nature in its own right were never visible. For the exercise of reason is a life, and every life involves a world to live in, a world appropriate to the exercise of that life.

Here is where I leave for the present the history of the soul. The last lecture in this series I plan to devote to the life of reason. There is, however, a remark to make as I conclude this one. It is now, I hope, clear, in spite of many obscurities in detail, of which I am unhappily conscious, that the psychology of Aristotle is wholly free from any separation of the soul from nature. It is wholly innocent, and I may say quite naively innocent, of those perplexing problems which worried later generations. It is innocent of epistemology. It is innocent of Augustinianism, Cartesianism, Lockianism, and Kantianism. It has not so set the mind over against nature, that the problem of how the mind can have anything to do with nature must first be solved before a man can have confidence in the operations of his intelligence. All this freedom is a consequence of beginning psychology with an inquiry into what the soul is. This linkage of the soul with nature, however, makes of the history of the soul an introduction to the history of nature at large. From psychology we go to physics and to metaphysics.

# III

## Physics and Metaphysics

The appropriate thing to say at the beginning of a lecture on the *Physics* of Aristotle is that his *Physics* is not physics at all. It is something else. It is a theory of nature, that system of things which allows a plant to grow, an animal to graze, and a man to think, fully as much as it allows the sun to be eclipsed or bodies to be in motion or at rest. It deals with space, time, and matter, and in that respect resembles physics, but it deals with them in a way that has shocked physicists for centuries. Accordingly, in dealing with Aristotle, one has to try the best one can to forget that there ever has been any physics at all. This is not easy. I am sure that I shall not succeed in that great act of forgetfulness, but I shall try. To assist me in this effort, I wish it to be remembered that my frequent use of the noun "physics" and the adjective "physical" is a usage in the Aristotelian manner. He has a good claim on them historically. They are Greek words. They are not translations of English, French, or German words. He is not responsible for their transliteration into other tongues nor for their use as names for an enterprise in which his writings show what he would call an accidental interest. This enterprise, so largely neglected in his writings, was none the less familiar to him. He performed, for example, an experiment to find the weight of air. He was versed in the mathematics and astronomy. I think he was a far better mathematician than Plato, even if Plato captured the greater reputation by exalting mathematics to the skies. He made a formula for the transfer of motion through contact. He was interested in mechanical devices. But when he composed his *Physics* he had a different enterprise in view than the one these illustrations suggest.

The book which is called the *Metaphysics* never had its title from Aristotle. It seems that early editors of his works, but more than two centuries after his death, put a collection of treatises after the *Physics* and named it for the sake of reference, "The books after the *Physics*." This was later shortened to "metaphysics." Thus a word was started on a momentous career in consequence of a piece of editorial nomenclature. I shall use the word from time to time for reference as the makers of it intended it to be used. I may use it sometimes because I like it, although in the sense in which I like it, it might just as well be called "before" as "after" physics. I find it difficult to distinguish it in any important way from the *Physics*. It may be distinguished by a fuller and more advanced treatment of some subjects which occur in the *Physics* and by a preliminary treatment of others. But I find it part and parcel of the same enterprise as that in which the *Physics* is engaged. Indeed there are several treatises of Aristotle which we have as apparently distinct, in the sense that they form different books, but which obviously belong together as contributions to the same general undertaking. (I may interject here the general comment that the titles of Aristotle's books are by no means free from the suspicion of editorial management. This is evident when they are compared with cross-references in the text.) This may be described as a theory of nature or a definition of what nature is. In dealing with this theory or definition, I shall try to present its salient features as I did in dealing with the history of the soul. Much will have to be omitted and many important critical questions ignored. Aristotle, as I have said, always brings his categories to bear on the matter in hand. He plays them off against each other. He solves many a difficulty by expressing his solutions in terms of them. All this is very bewildering to the reader and a splendid opportunity for the commentator. But there is a mass or total effect of it all. That, to my mind, is more interesting and perhaps more important than the suspected niceties of distinction in terminology.

But the noun "nature" and the adjective "natural" are troublesome although probably not more troublesome than they are with us. Aristotle repeatedly warns the reader that these words are used in several ways, five at least, and he is often careful to point out just how he uses them in particular passages. They are both technical and literary, technical, for example, when we speak of the nature of fire, literary when we say nature does nothing in vain, since for fire to be precisely what it is and not air or water is its nature, while there is no doer which we can identify as nature exclusively and which is free from variety. Whatever is done is never done without effect and since this is so in the case of every specific nature that can be identified, it is natural to say that nature does nothing in vain. One must get the feel of the language, so to speak, to understand it. When this is done, these words are found to vary from technical precision to literary convenience.

In what I have called a theory or definition of nature, they emphasize a distinction which Aristotle regards as very thought-provoking, the distinction between "nature" and "art." He gives many illustrations of it. He regards it as clearly evident and identifiable, and as the basal motivation of human inquiry. One of his illustrations is this: "If a house were naturally produced, it would be produced in the manner in which it is now produced by art. And if the things which are produced only by nature were also produced by art they would be produced in the manner in which they are produced by nature." (*Physics* 199a 13 f.) His meaning seems to me to be perfectly clear, and it would be a pity to cloud it by a dialectical discussion of the question whether art is not nature after all. Such discussions he was familiar with and would have none of except, when meeting dialecticians on their own ground, he turned their weapon against themselves. When he goes to work on his own account, it is sufficient for him to start with the observation that if a house came into being as a plant grows, we should call a house natural and a product of nature, and if a plant came into being as a house is built, we should call it artificial and a product of art.

From illustrations like this he goes to a formulation of the distinction in terms of his categories, but the distinction is identified before it is so transformed. The formulation is something like this: Nature is, or natural objects are, that which itself contains the determination of what it is or is to be, while art is, or artificial objects are, that which has this determination elsewhere. In the plant the determination is in the plant; in the house it is in the builder. The plant makes itself under the conditions of its making. This the house does not do. No distinction is to him clearer.[1] And this distinction defines for him the supreme problem of his system. Given the conditions under which a builder builds a house, it is manifestly easy to exhibit how the house is built. This we may generalize. We may say that given the conditions under which any experiment is performed by an experimenter, it is comparatively easy to analyze what happens in the experiment. This is not a statement translated out of Aristotle, but I am sure he would have put it in if he had thought of it, for it is what his illustrations and his use of them imply. All experimental inquiry is artful. It is, in effect, just like building a house. The experimenter takes his materials and sets up an experiment and observes what happens, and his experiments, especially his fruitful ones, are directed toward some problem in his mind. This is just what the builder of a house does. The builder must know something of mechanics if his house is to stand up and not fall down. He must know about stresses and strains. He must be something of a mathematician. He must weigh and measure. He must be familiar with

[1] In the margin here Woodbridge writes: "I cannot help here thinking of Darwin." His thought becomes explicit on pp. 145–46.

his materials, their strength, their resistance to heat and cold, their susceptibility to moisture and decay, and so on. The better he knows these things the better he can build. And he must also *want* to build in consequence of some inducement. The case is the same with the experimenter. The better he knows the characteristics of his materials and the better his command is of measuring and weighing, the better he experiments. And both do well when they know clearly what they are about.

But in nature as distinct from art, in that domain wherein situation after situation is disclosed wherein no builder or experimenter can be found, what are we to say? What are we to say of that domain in which there is no recognition of an outside control like that recognized in building or experimenting, and in which any outside control recognized is of quite a different sort and has always to be supplemented by something to which we give such names as "power," "energy," "force," "nature"? We are forever saying nature does this and that, nature does nothing in vain, nature is responsible. Sometimes it is nature at large, sometimes it is nature as fire, as life, as hydrogen, but where is the nature which does all this and who in the world ever identified it? We speak of the laws of nature, but who ever found this lawgiver? It is well to examine our habits of speech. Refine them as much as we will, there always lurks about them the shadow of the thought that nature works primarily as a builder or as an experimenter works. But nobody ever found the builder as one can find Phidias, nor the experimenter as one can find Daedalus.

So the great problem of Aristotle's system emerges: How is nature to be construed so that both the similarity and dissimilarity between its products and the products of art may be understood? It is clear now, I hope, why his *Physics* is so different from modern physics. Modern physics with all its achievements, could not, as I see it, modify that problem as a problem. It would certainly modify many of the particulars which Aristotle employed and modify some of them very radically indeed. But I cannot see that the problem itself would thereby be altered. He would have to speak of specific gravity instead of specific levity, but what difference would that make? He would have to speak of friction instead of fatigue; he would have to revise his distinction between the light and the heavy, the moist and the dry, the hot and the cold. He might not have to alter his conceptions of space and time or of matter. But it is difficult to see how such changes or freedom from change would alter his problem. This problem, I think, is just as statable today as it ever was. And I doubt if we are any wiser about the solution of it than he was.

His solution depends on giving to motion the central position in it. His theory of nature is a theory of motion. It starts with a generalization which was evidently a commonplace with all or nearly all of those men he calls the "physicists" of his own and earlier days. The passage from rest to motion, whenever it is observed, always requires a mover for its initiation. And this was usually supplemented by the further generalization that the mover itself must be in motion and initiates motion by contact. With these generalizations Aristotle starts, but insists that they necessarily involve the recog-

nition that motion is never anything apart from bodies and
that moving bodies are never apart from space and time. He
further insists that operating with moving bodies in space
and time, with a view to any quantitative determination of
them and their motions, carries one speedily to the infinite,
and often to a vacuum or the void. He rejects, however, the
theories of motion which are worked out in this setting, but,
so far as I can see, he rejects none of the facts on which they
are based. His reason for this wholesale rejection of the theories is based on three objections. The first I have already
mentioned, namely, that motion is not distinct from moving
bodies. Motion, that is, does not make bodies move. It is what
they do. There is no doubt at all that moving bodies by
moving make other bodies move, but to do this they must
first be in motion, with the consequence that motion is left
simply as a fact of observation to be dealt with as such, and
nothing more.

His second objection is that space, time, and the void are
nothing whatever apart from bodies. The analysis by which
he supports this objection will strike the modern reader as
astonishingly up to date. He rejects the void wholly and
utterly. He can find no evidence for it. With him it becomes
the same thing as nothing at all, and while he is willing to
admit that nothing at all may in some sense be said to be,
as when one says there is nothing at all in the pitcher, and
even when one says that beyond all things is nothing at all,
he cannot find that "nothing at all" is useful when one is
dealing with something else. The pitcher may indeed be
empty, but he is quite unwilling to admit that there is then

in it something which has dimensions which are not the dimensions of anything. As for space, he admits that the distinction between bodies and the place they occupy is thoroughly sound and readily made. Displacement is the proof of it, for one body may take the place of another. But there is no such thing as "space" in which this displacement occurs. Or, to put the matter in words more like his own, there is no place in which there are places for bodies to occupy. "Space" in any intelligible sense is, with him, only the fixation of the boundaries of bodies. The same fixation may be occupied by different bodies and two bodies may not occupy the same fixation, but the fixation itself does not occupy. Time is also distinguishable from bodies. They move with different speeds and we define speed as movement over a given place in a given time. Such expressions as "now," "earlier," "later," "before," "after," are meaningful expressions. They name the manner in which events occur. But there is no *time* in which they occur. That is, there is no independent scheme of before and after or of past, present, and future in which they occur. These distinctions of before and after and the like are consequences of the occurring of events, and this fact makes of time the number, measure, or order of these consequences. Nature is not somewhere in a void, nor is there an independent frame of space and time in which it is and in which its events take place.

His third objection is to the infinite. Here again is a remarkable piece of analysis. It is, I venture to suggest, well worth the attention of our mathematicians. His contention is that the infinite, although we meet it in many ways as when we divide a line, does not exist any more than space, time, or the void. Nature is not infinite nor in an infinite of any sort. The infinite is wholly a derivative of operations. We come upon it eventually; we cannot begin with it initially. We may speak of it as the possibility of performing operations of a certain kind, but should then remember that possibility has a variety of meaning and be careful which one we select. Our selection should be based on the fact that it is not the infinite which makes a line divisible, but it is the divisibility of the line which makes the infinite. And so in general: there is no infinity on which operations depend. Given the operations, however, infinity is discovered as something characteristic of them. The conclusion of his analysis may be summed up by saying: it is proper to speak of infinity and improper to speak of the infinite. An infinite line is wholly different from the infinity of a line.

After these objections there is little left beyond what we started with, namely, moving bodies and their mutual relations. There is profit in dealing with them in terms of space, time, and infinity, provided that space, time, and infinity are not turned into the fixed framework of nature. Moreover, the bodies themselves may be analyzed. As bodies they are reducible to the recognized elements earth, air, fire, and water. This is, however, too crude. The observed motion of these elements is such that some refinement upon them seems to be necessary. When we think of them in what may be called their purity, they always seem to be stratified with earth at the bottom and air or fire at the top. We speak here of bottom and top because any disturbance of this stratification is characterized by motion from or to earth. Each element thus tends to seek its proper place in relation to others. But the elements are never pure except when we think of them as wholly separated from each other. Earth and air are repeatedly moist, and fire consumes earthly things and dries the air. When we try now to bring all these considerations together we seem to be forced to recognize instead of earth, air, fire, and water something more primitive which we express in terms of the oppositions between the wet and the dry, the hot and the cold, and to find in these opposites the further distinction between the heavy and the light. This last distinction is also between up and down, for we say that the heavy sinks and the light rises. There is no absolute up and down, for this distinction is relative to that space or fixity of boundaries within which the motions of the elements take place. Every such space or fixity has its own up and down. In this manner Aristotle accounts for the appearance which the world presents to our observation. If there were time I would carry the account into some of its interesting details. There seems to be no doubt that Aristotle was, as we say, geocentric in his thinking, but it seems also true that he stated the geocentric position in a manner that freed it from an exclusively local interpretation. He stated it in terms of the idea of relative locality generalized. He objected to a multiplicity of local systems on observational and dialectical grounds. I often wonder what he would have said to later generations.

But the real problem of nature has not yet been touched. The motions we have been considering are evident enough, and they involve the distinctions which have been analyzed.

But the picture they give of nature is not that familiar scene which the sun shines upon and lets us see. To be sure we see moving things. They come and go. When, however, we say that a man goes from Athens to Thebes and comes back again, we have said the least significant thing about his journey. And he asks—or I make him ask in my imagination— Is it not the least significant thing to say about the sun's journey, that the sun goes round the earth? In going round the earth it makes successive places on the earth's surface visible. How poorly we should get on without that visibility! How little we should know about the world in which we live! By going round the earth, the sun divides day from night by casting a shadow on the sky, and by doing this provides a measure of time from which all other measures of it are derived. Without those measures where would history and astronomy be? By going round the earth, the sun puts things to sleep and wakes them up again. It wakes men up to the labors of the day, to the building of cities, to the business of politics, to the love of a good life, to the quest for knowledge, which quest is their chief dignity. By going round the earth, it quickens to life the most amazing company of plants and animals, which can be a source of endless curiosity and interest, with man the most endlessly curious and interesting of them all. By going round the earth, it affords an opportunity for the soul of man to gain that realm of being in which it is no longer the light of the sun that illumines, but the light of intelligence and mind.

Aristotle does not say all this in the way I have said it, but he says precisely the same thing in his categories. Occasionally he says something like it in the same way. And he does say that everything that happens on the earth is a consequence of movements that happen in the sky. We could call him an astrologer but should have to make him an astrologer without any superstition in him, or so little that it would be as readily forgiven as our own. I can imagine him, if that tradition is true which credits him with equaling and even surpassing Plato in style, I can imagine him writing without his precise categories and those characteristic algebraic expressions of his, writing in the language which men speak when they converse, go home or to the market place or the temple or the assembly. Such language he takes seriously and out of it he gets his categories. We have, I often suspect, lost the habit of taking it seriously. If, for example, facing a company of scientific men or even of those strange men who are called philosophers, I should tell them in all seriousness on my part that what the sun really does in going round the earth is to make available an intelligible world, would they applaud me for sanity or convict me of poetry or insanity? In the grip of Aristotle, I must, however, tell them just that and expect them to believe it.

But in that grip, I must tell them something far more incredible, far more poetic, far more insane, namely that what nature as a whole really is, what the most fundamental thing about it is, what—if I must use categories—what its "nature," its "essence," its "principle," its "law," its "order," its "system," is: what nature really is, is mind or intelligence in operation. Could poetry or insanity go further? Having let them go that far, we might, if we were still curious, pause to look at them with Aristotle's eyes instead of going home in amusement, pain, or disgust. A man who takes such things seriously may be said to be at least an interesting man. A poet like Dante is interesting, and he called Aristotle the master of them that know. And Aristotle happens to have been a man who could analyze space, time, and infinity in a rather masterful way, who knew more about animals than his successors knew for centuries, who collected the constitutions of Greek cities, who wrote on politics and ethics, and who wrote a book on poetry which critics are not yet tired of studying. All this combines to make an interesting circumstance in the history of human thought.

We need to be as naive as possible in dealing with this circumstance. I need to remind myself that I have suggested that Aristotle should be read in forgetfulness of what has happened since his day. Obviously I have not succeeded. So here I might recall an important thing that happened. Aristotle's doctrine of nature and his history of the soul, his Physics and his Psychology, if you will, cannot be separated. He may have gone from his Psychology to his Physics, but the effect of this was to make the Psychology a part of the Physics. We may accuse him of psychologizing nature, but that is something of which he is quite innocent in his own system. Our accusation rests on a totally different theory of the soul from his. This we must remember if we are to see in his Physics what he saw and not read into it an unwarranted transfer of psychological characters into the realm of nature.

One has only to read his *Psychology* and then read St. Augustine, Descartes, and John Locke to discover what a change had come over psychology by the time Locke wrote his *Essay Concerning Human Understanding*. And one has only to remember the name of William James and the names of men still living to be conscious of the desperate efforts psychologists have made to get out of the clutches of that essay and find for psychology a new principle. Locke did not and could not think of nature and the soul as Aristotle thought. Neither could the nineteenth century. For with Locke and for the nineteenth century the soul was quite unnecessary to the system of the world as a system. It was necessary if there was to be knowledge of that system, but so far as the system was concerned, it was necessary for nothing else. It could be blotted out without anything whatever happening to the system. It had its own peculiarities and its own career. These kept getting in its way when knowledge was its concern, and betrayed it into the bad habit of committing the pathetic fallacy, talking, that is, of nature as if it too had a soul and tried to do something as the soul tried. And the most unforgivable instance of this habit was the assigning to nature of powers and purposes. These shady things were symptoms of a psychological sickness which nature itself does not know. All this should be remembered. The soul was not the first entelechy of a natural organic body; it was a queer thing inside a man that thinks and feels and wills. In reading Aristotle the question which of these rival doctrines of the soul is right, need not be decided, but I am quite sure that this is sun clear, namely, that Aristotle can be convicted or acquitted of nonsense only in terms of the decision made. And it should further be remembered that Aristotle was familiar with something like the Lockian doctrine of the soul, and that he rejected it with all its implications. Remembering all this, perhaps one may go back to Aristotle forgetting that it ever happened.

Then it does seem that the discovery of what is intelligible in nature does largely depend on the sun's going round the earth, exposing to the eye things that can be examined, can be said to be thus and so, can be expressed in language, and find their articulations and connections in a system of categories. The further this examination is carried out, the more this saying thus and so is indulged in, the more this expression is made precise, and the more this articulation is found to be well-jointed, the more it appears that there is a power in nature in consequence of which the operations of nature are so much like the operations of art. It is this likeness which is the great problem which the consideration of nature sets. Just going back and forth will not do. The man does go from Athens to Thebes and the sun in a great sphere does go round the earth, swinging annually from north to south and back again, but the important thing in each case is the business which calls them to their journeys. The man's business is to build a house. The sun's business is to expose the doing of things so obviously similar. The man was attracted to build the house by such desirable things as comfort, better living, or financial profit (and comfort, better living and financial profit are quite possible to attain in a world like this). Is not the sun also attracted to make its exposition by something also desirable and possibly attainable? Are not all genuinely genetic processes, processes, that is, which issue in results which strike one immediately as the end or consummation of those processes, are they not all motivated at last by the pressure in the system of things, of something ultimately to be desired and which evokes desire to be like it, so that each thing in nature aims at what we call its appropriate good?

It is such a picture of nature that the reader may get when he puts the *Physics* and *Metaphysics* together and takes nature out of the categories of Aristotle and talks about it in terms of soul and body, plants, animals, and men, building houses, making statues, turning stones into doorsteps, going to and from Athens, seeing with the eye and hearing with the ear, getting sick and getting well, turning pale and turning red, a child becoming a man and a man a general, Socrates' snub nose, Coriscas's peculiarities, the shining sun and night with its stars, instead of in terms of principle, element, substance, quantity, quality, relation, place, time, situation, condition, action, passion, accident, privation, material cause, formal cause, efficient cause, final cause, motion, potentiality, actuality, realization, entelechy, and *noesis*. It does no harm to put it back again into the categories. Indeed Aristotle seems to have thought that by putting it into categories one would have to see it and could also silence those who blotted out the vision of it, particularly men like Empedocles and Democritus, and those who obscured and confused the vision of it, men like Plato. So some acknowledgment of the categories may be made, and here, going back to motion, some of them may be made to reappear.

Aristotle shifts emphasis from the moving body, where it was usually put, to the body moved, where it was not usually put. Of course, it is possible to say that the body at rest is

moved out of its state of rest by the moving body which impinges upon it. The moving body is the mover, the efficient
cause or factor of the second body's moving. But the fact that
the second body moves cannot be disregarded. His analysis of
motion denied that motion is something apart from bodies,
something which can be passed from one body to another, as
a man can pass his coat to another man. The second body's
motion is not the first body's motion, but its own. He regards
this fact as amply supported both by observation and argument. Obviously there never was a time when there was no
motion, since the analysis of time showed that time is the
measure of motion, and consequently without motion there
can never be the "never was" of time. But if the motion of the
second body is not its own, then the motion of the first body
is not its own either, and we are forced to conceive an endless
series of motions or a continuity of motion. The latter cannot
be the motion of any distinguishable body, and consequently
never an efficient cause or factor, and the former would make
the motion of bodies impossible, because its demand for an
endless series of prior motions could never be satisfied by a
first moving body. This is what I make out of his argument
to prove that the motion of the second body is just as much
its own as the motion of the first is its own. In following the
argument it is necessary to remember that with him anything
like absolute and infinite space, time or motion has disap-
peared.

Now, then, if the motion of the second body is its own and
the second body moves from the situation of rest to the situation of motion, the second body must have the power to do

this. That this power is not sufficient to make it move is evident enough. And if it were enough it would not need an efficient cause or factor to release its power. But its power is not to be denied. The recognition of its power is the recognition that nature is essentially dynamic, that it is a realm of powers, and motion now, whenever we think of the start or beginning or principle of motion, is always a passage from what can be to what is, a passage from potentiality to actuality, from δύναμις to ἐνέργεια, or, as one might say in homely language, from power (ability) to work. The start or beginning of motion is, therefore, not something that happened only once in the dim and distant past; it happens just when it happens and at no other time. This passage from potentiality to actuality is what-motion-has-in-the-end, its realization or entelechy. It may now be said that potentiality is prior to actuality, δύναμις to ἐνέργεια, but this priority cannot be a spatial or temporal priority, it can be only a logical priority. Without it motion is unintelligible. To have motion intelligible there must be a logos of it, and without that logos it would not occur, any more than Socrates could be put to death without a syllogism which defines the logos of his mortality.

But the actual must also be in some sense prior to the potential, for it is always some actually moving body which is the efficient cause or factor in promoting motion in some other body. The priority here, however, is not like that in the other case. Here it is temporal and not logical priority. It is a fact of observation and not the result of the reasoned consideration of the observation. So we have Aristotle's general definition of physical motion: such motion is strictly not spatial, but dynamic change, a passage from potentiality to actuality, with the start or principle of motion in the body which moves; with the potentiality of motion logically prior to its actuality and actual motion temporally prior to the potential. It is clear that he is defining motion in terms of his conviction that the distinction between "what *can* be" and "what *is,*" which common speech is constantly making, is natural, not only in the mouths of men, but also in the processes of nature. With him it is a real distinction before it is a verbal one, and, indeed, could not be the verbal one it is unless nature supported it. Without it, he cannot comprehend nature in any intelligible way, for without it he finds that space, time, infinity, and moving bodies, with all of which the physicist deals, involve him in absurdities. One is the absurdity of absolute space as a place in which there is a place in which the world resides. A second is that there is an absolute time wherein there is a moment, or an hour, or a day, or a great stretch of years, in which the duration of the world is dated. A third is that there is the absolute infinite which none the less has parts, which make the capture of a tortoise by Achilles impossible. And a fourth is that there must be a procession of moving bodies without a first moving body in the procession. All these he thinks are absurdities out of which the mind of man can make no sense whatever. From them he finds escape in a wholly dynamic conception of motion, in the conception of it as the release of power, in the conception of it as the passage from what can be to what is.

It is this dynamic or generative emphasis which is the dominant characteristic of the Aristotelian system as a whole. It is, perhaps, best understood when put in contrast to the system which he principally opposed, namely the system represented by Empedocles and Democritus. These men, as he represents them to us, did acknowledge forces, the former a combining force called "love" and a separating force called "hate," and the latter a force called "necessity," which in some respects was not a force at all, but only a name for what inevitably follows from defined conditions, as when we say that given the definition of a circle, its diameters are equal by necessity. All these forces did, however, was to bring about arrangements and rearrangements of elements which were themselves changeless, as one might arrange and rearrange the letters of the alphabet.

Aristotle insisted not only that this conception of things involved difficulties about space, time, and infinity which made it ultimately unintelligible, but also that nature was patently not that kind of a system. Nature, instead of presenting such arrangement and rearrangement as its chief characteristic, presents rather a development, a genuinely generative process, the successive coming into being of products which are clearly different from their origin. Like art, nature is a producer; to use his own illustration, nature is like a builder, and although building does involve the arrangement of given materials by employing the force of the builder, and although the resulting structure may exhibit necessary relations between its parts, the product is a house, and houses may be very different from one another.

Empedocles and Democritus give us nature without its differences or with those differences only which can be numerically expressed. The significant and challenging thing about nature is, however, to be constantly different from what it was, and different in a way not at all definable in terms of quantity and number, but in terms of such things as houses, plants, animals, men and stars. And, further, it is only distinctions of this latter sort that really do distinguish. Even the distinctions of quantity and number are distinctions of this sort, for in a pile of apples we distinguish "pile" and "apples" and "number" and "large" and "small." All these distinctions are *within nature,* not *between natures.* We cannot separate them as with a knife and then put them together again into a pile of apples, for number and pile and apples are not separable in that fashion. To be sure, a number of apples may be brought together in a pile, but then it is a "pile of apples" that we have and not "a number" or "a pile" or "an apple." Nature is not like combinations by "love" and "hate" of earth, air, fire, and water, nor combinations by the "necessity" of moving atoms; it is like a seed becoming a plant, a child a man, a man a general, or a stone a doorstep. Nature is a dynamic and productive system, not a static system disturbed now and then by forces which rearrange its parts.

Aristotle is opposed to Plato also, or to Plato as he conceives him. Plato recognized the shortcomings of such men as Empedocles and Democritus, but what he substituted for them was wholly visionary. For Plato, to keep the homely illustration of the apples, thought that there were, independent of matter, realities like "pile" and "number" and "apple," which by their own creative power took up residence, so to speak, in matter, and so made a pile of apples. He was not quite so gross as this because his interest being mainly in morals and politics, his perfect essences were more refined and were ultimately "the good," but whenever he turned to nature, he carried over into it his moral habit, made the good take up a parceled residence in matter and even made "the great" and "the small" creative or manufacturing principles. Aristotle insists on "essences" as confidently as does Plato, but he insists also that they are to be dynamically construed and thought of as what matter energized can exhibit. They are not fragmented, reflected or shadowed visitors from heaven. Plato is too imaginative to be taken seriously.

Aristotle's own consciousness of these two oppositions is one of the clearest things in his writings. When he looks at nature, he does not see earth, air, fire, and water operated upon by love and hate, attraction and repulsion; he does not see atoms moving necessarily in a void; he does not see heavenly essences reflected in a refracting mirror; he sees the obvious and insists that nature must first be defined in terms of the obvious before we proceed to any theory of nature. We must say first "what nature is," and then we must say that nature is a producer of products so like the products of art that nature must be construed after the manner of such products. It must be construed as the use of materials to produce what can be produced out of them. Metaphysics, if you will, must precede Physics, or nature, rendered first in terms of its obvious genetic processes, must precede any other rendering of it and be basic to other renderings. This is the main thing. To begin in any other way is to muddle all subsequent procedure.

If this is clearly understood, then his adding on to the efficient cause and factor those other factors, the material, the formal, and the final, which came later to be called "causes" also, is a procedure not so wanton as it might otherwise appear to be. Into these so-called causes I have not time to go at much length. I prefer to call them "factors," for "cause" is a term Aristotle never used. Nor did he use the term "factor" for that matter, but since he is dealing with products and productivity, I find the term "factor" less misleading. A product implies factors, and so in examining a product the first thing to do is to examine the factors of it. There is the material factor like the stones and timbers of a house; there is the formal factor, like that which the word "house" designates and distinguishes a house from a barn; there is the final factor which is the use, service, or end which the house illustrates; and there is the efficient factor which is the builder of the house. All these factors, thinks Aristotle, are distinguishable in every product of nature just as they are in every product of art. And they all involve, taken together and taken simply, a passage from potentiality to actuality. If we can speak of a framework, the framework of nature is now defined as he defined it. From this we may proceed, and as we proceed we find different branches of knowledge arising to clarify nature's productivity, but we never find a science which can displace what the physics and the metaphysics primarily reveal. There is a "first philosophy" which is prior to every other "philosophy."

The "first philosophy," however, raises a problem about which all men ultimately speculate. The parallelism between nature and art is quite sufficient for the development of the knowledge of nature's processes as they actually occur. It is the business of knowledge to find out the four factors in the specific products of nature and to refine upon them as much as possible. As I have said, different branches of knowledge are necessary for this. These all go together to form a system of knowledge under the control of the first philosophy. But this philosophy raises about nature at large the same question it raises about nature in detail. And here the parallelism with art breaks down. To speak about nature at large or nature as whole is, with Aristotle, to speak about something definite and precise, all that the boundary of which is the sky, all that which is in the sky without the sky's being in something else. We must constantly remember that with him there is no absolute space beyond the heavens or the sky. There the "all" stops. I do not think that this means with him quite what we mean when we say that the universe is "finite," for with him a finite as distinct from an infinite universe means nothing. We have to try to think in following him that with the sky we have all the universe there is, so that, if we went to the sky we should not find ourselves looking out into an endless distance whither we might go if there were something to go on; we should find ourselves rather going round the sky without any surprise at all. "Here" and "there" are distinctions only within the universe, and never between within it and without. So Aristotle's "all" or universe or "cosmos" is quite concretely complete and self-contained. But it provokes the problem of its own motion.

This motion as observed is circular. The astronomers have

conceived it in terms of spheres that move in great circles around the earth, carrying with them the heavenly bodies. These motions are endless, for being circular they are always complete and always returning on themselves, so that there is no place at which they can be said to begin or end. From these endless motions all the ending motions of nature are derived, but how? That they are effective is clear enough to observation, for there are all sorts of heavenly occurrences, the sun's heat, the seasons, the alternation of day and night, and upon such occurrences as these follow many others so that the earth responds with its countless activities. But Aristotle finds it difficult to admit that all this could ever occur just of itself. It is all too much like a work of art with no artist to do the work. Why do these heavenly spheres keep endlessly revolving? They are not pushed about and they clearly do not push themselves. They are the power to move endlessly actualized. But their power is not enough to move them because no power ever moves of itself. If it did everything that could be done would already have been done. Power would have exhausted itself. These endless motions need a mover, but it has to be a different sort of mover from them, a different sort in fact from any efficient cause. The mover is God. But how can he move the heavenly spheres without being another heavenly sphere, and so in need of another god? This is the problem. And this much of a solution is already suggested. God must move the heavenly spheres without touching them, without pushing them, without himself moving. He must be an unmoved mover. This is what the situation demands.

Here I leave Aristotle's theological problems for the present to return to it in the next lecture. Let me restate it in summary form. Aristotle finds nature to be a wholly self-contained system and a closed system in all respects save one. This one is observed when we compare the products of nature with the products of art. Both these products are externally, so to speak, of precisely the same sort. But we know that the products of art imply intelligence as their ultimate source. It seems impossible to say that nature also is the product of intelligence and mean what we mean when we speak of art. Yet without intelligence somehow present in nature, the release of power in the way it is released seems impossible. God seems to be necessary, but he cannot be necessary as the artist is necessary, who takes a block of marble and changes it into a statue of Hermes. Plants and animals and men do not become plants and animals in that way. Nothing natural becomes what it is in that way. Yet everything natural becomes what it is precisely as if that was the way of its becoming. Some method of God's working must be found which does not turn him into a man with a chisel and a hammer.

# IV

## The Life of Reason

Santayana has done a service to the language by transforming a phrase of Aristotle's into the title of a profound and beautiful book, naming the book *The Life of Reason*. The expression is to be taken quite literally and not figuratively or metaphorically. And Santayana has condensed the meaning of it into one of his unforgettable sentences by saying of Aristotle: With him, "Everything ideal has a natural basis and everything natural an ideal development."[1] This is true of man, whose life begins humbly, much like the life of a plant, with little more than the need of food, which is supplied him naturally, and rises to the exercise of his reason, with its need of the food of knowledge. For this need there is also provision in nature. She has not been so forgetful, one might say, that after providing air and sunlight, bread and butter, which can

[1] George Santayana, *The Life of Reason:* Vol. I, *Reason in Common Sense* (New York, 1905), p. 21.

be had without effort or with a little industry, she has left man's mind hungry with nothing to feed on. "For the exercise of reason is also life," says Aristotle. It is quite inconceivable to him that the wants of the stomach should find appropriate satisfactions in the world in which it is, but the wants of the mind should find none.

Nature does nothing in vain. Even in inanimate things there is a nice adjustment to conditions. Earth, air, fire, and water behave in ways which look as if they were provided for them. At least, we find out these ways, and having found them out exclaim: "How natural it is for the elements to behave that way!" And how natural it is for the fish to swim, the bird to fly, and the snake to glide! Such things may appear to be wonders and marvels at first, miracles forever surprising. They are not such, however, after they have been examined. Then they are natural. Indeed—and this is Aristotle's own remark—the ignorant man is surprised because the diagonal and side of a square are incommensurable, but the geometer would be surprised if they were not. This elimination of surprise by the understanding of nature's behavior is what we mean when we say that nature does nothing in vain. In her domain there seems to be provision for whatever happens—provision, indeed, for whatever can happen, so that if something does not happen, that is, perhaps, more difficult to explain than anything that does. We are forced to suspect some resistance and stubbornness somewhere, some intractability, and find this either in the stubbornness or inertia of matter, or in the fact that events fall out as it were and get in the way of each other, as a man may go from Athens to Thebes and be robbed on the way, suffering thus by accident rather than by nature. It was not the nature of his journey to be robbed. It is thus either the inertia of matter or the effect of chance that interferes with the natural course of events.

Now, in the face of such ample provision, a provision which at first looks miraculous and at last admirable and fitting, nature would be convicted of vanity supreme, if man were left with a mind strangely isolated, a freak in an otherwise freakless world. But the exercise of reason is also life, and life literally. It is life fully as much as the exercise of the legs or of the stomach. As man's walking and digesting are exercises in conformity with the conditions in the world in which they are performed, so also is his thinking an exercise of the like character. The plant grows from seed to flower, finding an appropriate environment every step of the way. So a man grows from appetite to reason. He finds an appropriate environment for the lowest in him and also for the highest. If there is a movable world with its space, time, matter, and infinity, a nourishing world with its air, heat, food, and drink, a sensible world with its colors, sounds, tastes, and the like, there must also be an intelligible or logical world with its categories, its logoi, yes, even its syllogisms. It is by living, really living, in such a world that a man thinks. This thinking is just as much conformity with an intelligible world as his perceiving is conformity with a perceptible world, or his digestion is conformity with a digestible world. Nature does nothing in vain: and it would be absurd to suppose that in man, the life of reason, alone, depended only on himself or his soul. It depends on something else, and something else just as much not himself as his eating depends on something not himself.

So we must return to the history of the soul. For the exercise of reason is also life. It is man's highest life. We call it the highest because, just as vision goes up at last to the sky to find there its end or termination, so the soul of man goes up at last to reason to find in its life an ultimate satisfaction. It is also man's best life, for just as we call any life good, as the life of appetite or sense, when it reaches, as we say, its goal or finds the good at which it aims—and that at which anything aims is its good—so we call that life the best which is the soul's completest realization and fulfillment, and in which the soul has rounded out its history, found its good, and become intimate with its aim. It is a divine or godlike life, because an intelligible and logical world is not a world of material bodies but a world of ideas, of objects which are handled only by thought and seen only by what we call metaphorically the mind's eye. Then, there is light indeed, not the light which ever was on sea or land, but that light which illumines sea and land and all that they contain in such a way that they can be known and understood.

This, Aristotle's conception of reason as life, when thus expressed in our own familiar words, may sound like what we call poetry. With him, however, it is all quite literal. His own language, in dealing with it, often becomes elevated and moving. He would, if asked, have explained this by saying that the subject-matter was such that only such language was appropriate. If he should use that category of ours which makes the robust claim to truth, he would say that it was all thoroughly "scientific." That is, he had no doubt about it. The soul of man does grow from the fertilized seed in the mother's womb to the full stature of a man of science. This is its natural history. Around this history grow up all human institutions, the household, the city, the school, the temple, the games, the theater. And agreeable to these institutions are such branches of knowledge as economics, ethics, politics, rhetoric, and poetics. The natural history of the soul is back of them all, and the law of that history is: as perception is to the perceived, so is thought to the thought-of. We can turn the elevated expression of it all into an algebraic formula. It is well to do this, for doing it is a reminder that there are in nature realms of being in which life may be lived and lived well. These realms of being correspond to the development of the soul, and its development corresponds to them. In its development it is constantly being informed by them and constantly seeking conformity with them, troubled only by the inertia of matter and the subjection to chance. These, however, a man may, by study and exercise and by a wise administration of his affairs, in some measure control.

In leading the life of reason, by being in the intellectual world, the soul finds itself freed from bodily limitations. No longer is it limited to the place where the body is, or the time which measures the body's motion. These it is free from. Its power here, although a power which it could not exercise without a body to support it, is not a bodily power. Its failing, for it is often said to fail, is like the failing of perception, not a failing in the power, but in the organ, as a man sees poorly when his eyes grow old and weak. The failing of the power of reason is like that, but the power itself comes from that intellectual world in which the life of reason is lived. At the summit of the natural history of the soul, that history is

somehow reversed. Something enters the soul from without—
θύραθεν is the word, as if a visitor came in from out of doors.
The visitor is both important, and occasional. It is only in
those brief moments when life is at its best that he is genuinely present and his power observed in its effectiveness. At
other times when, because of the body, the soul is busy with
practical affairs, the visitor may be a stranger. When, however,
he is present, the life of reason is no longer practical. It becomes theoretical or speculative, and this is what makes the
visitor important.

These words "theoretical" and "speculative" have to be
taken out of the familiar context in which we use them and
put in another. We must remember that with the Greeks,
"theoretical" was an adjective derived from the uses of the
theater, and not from those of a scientific laboratory or of a
study. The emphasis falls on beholding, on the vision before
one, on the vision of something one beholds without taking
part in what one beholds. The sense of it is readily had in a
theater. There we behold a spectacle, and by beholding it are
moved to laughter or tears. The spectacle—we might say, in
tune with Greek usage, the "theory," the thing "theorized" or
beheld—works upon us in a different fashion from the fashion of the builder who works upon the materials of his house.
Yet the fashion is not wholly different, for examining the
builder more closely than when we observe only the working
of his hands, we find that the idea of the house he is building
is the prime mover of what he builds. It is due to its presence
and his beholding of it that the materials of the house go
together as they do, hindered only by their matter and by the

chances which beset a building operation. This idea moves other things without being moved or moving itself. It moves not by pushing, but, as it were, by attracting. It is as if its bare presence in a world of men who can build and of materials that can be built into a house, changed that "can be" into an "is," and so converted a potentiality into an actuality. And so the soul when that "theoretical" or speculative visitor is present seems at last to have found the prime mover of its whole natural history. In consequence of its attraction, the body has grown to be its residence for a season, and been hindered only by the inertia of matter and the vagaries of chance. Because of these hindrances souls stop part way in becoming what a soul can be. Yet each seems to be desiring to be more than it is. Indeed, all nature seems now to be like the movement of desire toward the desired. "Even the stone," says Aristotle, letting his imagination run a little wild, "desires to become a doorstep, and all things strive somehow after the divine."

It is in the psychology, in that reversal of the look of history which the supreme theoretical life of reason reveals, that Aristotle finds the clue to his answer to his theological question. Reason at its highest, and simply by being at its highest, releases power, just as the idea of the house, simply by being in the builder's mind when he builds, releases it. Here is an unmoved mover, and it makes the whole genetic process from nutrition to reason look different from the way it looked before. It looks now fully as much attracted by an active exercise in the realm of ideas as it is pushed by those efficient and pushing factors which play upon the body. There is the realm of ideas, which is not a bodily realm, and there is life there which is not a bodily life. Such a life, wholly free from any body, is what God is. "On such a start," says Aristotle, "heaven and earth depend. His life is always such as is ours in those brief moments when our life is at its best." He moves the heavenly spheres, not by pushing them about, turning himself into an efficient factor and a moving body; he moves them as the intellectual realm of being with its ideas moves the soul, as theory moves practice, as the seen play moves the audience, or as the lover is moved by the object of his love. His presence gives to the passage from power to act those countless illustrations in nature of aiming at a good, and to all genetic processes the attainment of those entelechies which now look like the reasons for their being at all. The processes of nature, looked at from the point of view of their historical order, look like a movement toward the divine, hindered only by chance and matter; looked at from the point of view of the divine, the divine becomes the first mover of them all. There is a kind of reciprocity between beginning and end, so that in the end, everything is what it was to be in the beginning.

It is God, then, that moves the heavenly spheres, the intellectual which is the ultimate source of motion. But the astronomers tell us there are fifty or more heavenly spheres. Shall we then have fifty or more gods? Aristotle is content with a line from Homer: "Things do not like to be misgoverned; let there be one commander."

I have tried to present Aristotle's theories of the soul and of nature, and his tying them together in his theology, all within

the limits set by his own body of knowledge and information.
I make no effort to free them from these limitations. He is
interesting enough without adding such an attempt. And
perhaps the most interesting thing about him is that notion
of "realms of being" appropriate to the exercises of the soul,
of life, lived now as a plant lives, in a world where food can
be had, now as an animal lives, in a world where there are
objects of perception which can be remembered and employed,
and now as the rational man lives, in a world of ideas which
is the source of understanding, and which gets over into
language, so that men believe that by the use of words, by
sayings of one sort and another, they can tell themselves and
others what things are and what nature is. This is impressive.
As I read the history of philosophy, it is not until I come to
Spinoza in the seventeenth century that I find anything
really comparable.

Perhaps I should now put all that I have been saying in a
fluid and discursive way back into the categories of Aristotle.
This, however, I refrain from doing, because I have, I hope,
given sufficient illustration of that method. The categories do
no more than provide a short and nicely knit way of saying
the same things. Yet in the matter of the theology, I may use
one of our own categories, drawn from chemistry, which
affords an analogy with Aristotle. In certain chemical situations, chemical action of a specific kind seems not to take
place unless there is present an activating agent. This agent
seems to do nothing in the situation beyond being present.
It is called a "catalyzer." It causes motion, apparently, without
being itself moved or in motion. It is like an unmoved mover.

Now it might be said that Aristotle found nature in need of a "catalyzer," an activating principle. With him this principle is not chemical; it is logical or intellectual. It does not create; it "catalyzes." The way it influences is like the way a clear idea influences the development of a theme, or a motif in music influences the development of a symphony.

It is usual to begin expositions of Aristotle with his classification of knowledge instead of with his history of the soul. I have begun with the latter because of the way he begins that history, and also because I find it illuminates both his procedure and his solution of the problems he raised. It affords also, as it is carried out with his other treatises, the basis for his classification of knowledge. His own division was into the theoretical, the practical and the poetic. I have dealt thus far with the theoretical. I should not leave the others without a comment.

The three kinds of science are distinguished by their aims and by their certainty. The aim of the theoretical is knowledge, of the practical behavior, and of the poetic composition. Since the theoretical deals with what happens always or usually it can claim certainty. The practical and the poetic, because their aim is either behavior or production(construction), imply something to be done, and are, consequently, not properly judged by such criteria as certainty or truth. They are judged rather by their effectiveness in disclosing the means best adapted to bring what is to be done to a fortunate or successful conclusion. Rules of conduct and rules of art are manuals for guidance rather than expositions of truth. They presuppose also some experience of life, for it is this experience which is really their subject-matter. One must, therefore, have had some experience, indeed considerable experience, before one ventures upon the study of them or the attempt to contribute to them worthily. There is a passage in the *Nicomachean Ethics* on which I have often pondered: "A man," Aristotle says, "is a good judge of what he understands, and good in proportion to his experience. The young, therefore, are not fit students of Politics, because they are inexperienced in those actions of life which are the subject-matter of this branch of knowledge. Besides, since they follow their emotions, they will study vainly and without profit, for the aim of Politics is not knowledge but action. And it makes no difference whether one is young in years or in character, for the defect is not due to time, but to living and acting emotionally. To such persons, knowledge is as useless as it is to the intemperate." (*Ethics* 1095a 1 f.)

The practical sciences comprise economics, ethics, and politics, and the poetical the various arts and technologies. We have from Aristotle treatises on the former, but of the latter little more than his *Rhetoric* and *Poetics*. Although these sciences which deal with behavior and construction are not theoretical, they have a basis in theory. It is this feature of them which, in the study of Aristotle, is probably more interesting and important than the details which bear directly on performance. I illustrate this from the *Poetics* and the *Ethics*.

Aristotle's treatise on poetry is clearly a guide for poets, intended to help them to write poetry well. Its advice is based on the successful accomplishments of the celebrated poets of Greece. The warning, which I noted in that quotation from the *Ethics,* is observed. One must have read a good deal of Greek poetry if one is properly to understand the advice, and one evidently must have both ability and a decent theme, to follow the advice with profit. The treatise is not intended to produce poets or to cause discussion of the poetic temperament. One might venture to say that it is not even a theory of poetry, although there is theory in it, some attempt to make one see what poetry is. In the first place, poetry is identified not so much by its form as by its subject-matter. Empedocles wrote in verse, but might just as well have written in prose. He is distinguished from Homer, who was a poet, by having a different subject-matter, namely, nature and not the actions of men. These latter give to poetry its themes. Yet poetry differs from history. "For it is the work of the poet to tell, not what happened, but such things as might happen in all likelihood or necessity. The historian and the poet do not differ by speaking, the one without verse and the other with it, for Herodotus could be put into verse, but would be no less history with verse than without it; they differ by speaking, the one of what has happened, the other, of what might happen. Wherefore poetry is more philosophical and more serious than history." (*Poetics* 1451a 36 f.) Poetry makes us see men and their actions against the background defined by human possibilities, with chance and fate seen to be cooperating factors in their destinies and careers—not men walking about the streets or attending to their business with chance and fate unattended to, but man himself, portrayed in characters of men better or worse than men usually are, and so portrayed that human nature may be beheld in the clutch of circumstance and as a spectacle over against the deeds of men simply recorded as events. There we get a more serious or more philosophical view of the realities and entanglements of human life than we can from an account of what actually happened.

Thus it is its subject-matter that gives to poetry its definition and its character. And herein is discovered the effect it has on the mind, the effect, namely, of a kind of liberation or catharsis. There is what might be called a natural preparation for this effect. We find pleasure in play, dance, picturings, and pageantry. They are both delightful and instructive. We learn from them just as children take their first lessons from pictures. Indeed, pictures generally have an interesting effect, which is emphasized when the picture is of something horrible. The horrible thing in reality we would avoid, avoid even looking at it. But we will look at pictures of it and with a certain fascination, as if we were learning from it. And, says Aristotle, it is always a joy to learn, perhaps man's most characteristic joy. It gives him the pleasure of saying that things are thus or so, and enhances his sense of power and detachment.

Poetry springs from this natural basis. It is the technical or artistic development of it by means of mimicry or representation through the use of appropriate materials like sound, rhythm, color, and the stage. It enhances the natural effect of representations. It reaches its culmination in tragedy, for tragedy is the highest and most serious form of poetry. Here the actions of men are portrayed by the use of a technique which is designed to bring before the spectator a balanced representation, by which the characters in the tragedy are controlled without their knowledge, but which the technique enables the beholder to be conscious of and understand. The play is one thing for the actors and quite a different thing for the spectator. It is as if the actors were living men, playing their parts in life, unconscious of their fate, while the spectators see them caught in their fate, and laugh or cry at the spectacle.

The spectators *do* nothing about the action. They only behold it. In beholding it they have their laughter and tears, their pity and fear. But their pity and fear has been freed from those natural causes which produce these emotions in daily life. They are sublimated, we might say. And this sublimation works in the beholder as theoretical knowledge works. It gives him the sense of freedom from the very emotions he has felt. The freeing of these emotions from the natural causes from which they normally spring has wrought an intellectual detachment from them. Although the spectators laugh and cry, they have, by beholding a spectacle, passed beyond laughter and tears. In them pity and fear have been aroused only to be transformed into a purification or catharsis. To laugh and to cry, and yet at the same time to be beyond laughter and tears, is both to know these emotions and to be free from them. Tragedy brings this about, and the beholders of tragedy enjoy it. But it is not laughter and tears which they enjoy. It is, rather, a godlike sense of superiority to them.

Let the reader of the *Poetics* go to the theater and check up the analysis of Aristotle with his own experiences. I think they will match. Let him recall that moment at the end of a good play, the moment before the applause comes to shatter it, or a neighbor's remark brings back the active world. I think he will find it a moment when the sense of life's complications is very high, and freedom from them equally high. It is not the freedom of the disinterested spectator, for interest has been a matter of laughter and tears. It is not the freedom of the egotistic spectator, who is glad that he is not what he has seen. It is wholly a different sort of freedom from either of these. It is a freedom of a soul freed from laughter and tears, yet knowing what they are because he has shared them. When that moment is shattered, something very supreme has gone away. Such precious moments all great art has the power to add to the wayward moments of an all too passionate life.

The matter may be carried further. Art, says Aristotle, is an imitation of nature. It is necessary here to remember the history of the soul and the doctrine of nature which culminated in a theology, if one is not to be led astray by that word "imitation." Art does not simply make things that look like nature. It *does,* either in fact or in semblance, what nature does in reality. It imitates the process or method of nature, does something like that. This is clearly seen in the physician's art. By imitating the processes of nature which keep men well, he makes a sick man well. Art is thus a kind of perfecting of nature, or a remedying of its defects. It is at bottom an overcoming or elimination of that stubbornness of matter and those disturbances of chance which twist nature, as it were, out of its usual or proper course. Art provides this overcoming or elimination when it can, and when it cannot it creates the semblance of it. So the products of art find a natural criticism in their congruence with nature. They must always be what nature might produce if it could, but what it might produce free from the impediments in its way. They must represent nature at its best in whatever is represented. If they cannot produce reality, they must produce the semblance of it. Otherwise that supreme effect of art is lost. This demand upon the products of art gives to this effect the definition of its proper character. It may now be seen as the effect which fully successful living would produce. If a man could so control his living that he rises to those moments when his life can be viewed as a spectacle, and yet viewed with that freedom or purification which the theater can reveal, he would have controlled his life well. He would be a wise man, a philosopher. To get such moments is the supreme aim of human life. Art is a revelation of such moments. The life of reason is the practical exercise which may reach them through the control of the soul's natural development.

The *Ethics* of Aristotle looks like a guide to this end. Its theme is how to live well. Nature provides for living. It provides even for getting angry. Anybody can get angry. That's easy. But with whom? How much? When? What for? And how? That's not easy. (1109a 26) Persons, amounts, occasions, purposes, methods—it is just such things as these which make the difference between living and living well. Right behavior is a discipline of natural behavior. Nothing natural is in itself wrong, for everything natural is an exhibition of nature's powers. To pass from the natural to the right is to pass from living to that art of living which we call ethics.

And ethics, as the word implies, is a matter of the habits, customs, rules of conduct, and characters of men. It implies community, the sense of sharing in good and evil, just and unjust; and so, although it has to do with men as individuals, it has to do with them as individuals in families and in cities. Ethics is consequently a branch of politics. It presupposes society. It emphasizes the fact that really to live well, one must not live in isolation but in a community. It is hardly a compliment to call a man good if he is not of a family or a city, if he has no friends or enemies. Such isolation likens him to a beast or a god. To be fully a man, to live well as a man, he must actively participate in the lives of men.

There are other conditions for well-being, at least for living well supremely. A child, for example, may live well as a child, but its life is hardly one to choose as an example. Long life, a life which passes from childhood to maturity, can furnish a much better example, the example, indeed, which sets a standard. And this should be remembered in the training of children. Nature can see to their becoming old, but art must see to their becoming old well. As one swallow or one day does not make a spring, so a short life does not make a fortunate or happy man. To long life should be added other conditions for the complete picture, beauty, health, wealth, family distinction. It may be noted that the great poets deal with great families. (Book I, ch. 6) Things like these are more than desiderata. They set standards. They make of ugliness, disease, poverty, and lack of distinction things to disquiet the statesman. It is not well simply to accept them or say that they make no difference in living well. To be sure a man may live as well as he can and be so far forth admirable without them; but he is then living as well as he can, not as well as life might be lived in better circumstances. It is rather a desperate ethic, thinks Aristotle, and one wholly subversive to sound political institutions, which takes its standard from misfortune. The unfortunate do not set the standard of citizenship—neither slaves nor those who toil. Philanthropy is medicine, but not morals. Only a lack of intelligence confuses them.

There is another condition of living well which troubles Aristotle. He was an observer of men and things. He wrote his *Ethics* conscious of much discussion of the subject. He set himself squarely against the doctrine which was associated with the names of Socrates and Plato and which held that *knowledge* was at the bottom of the good life, that no man willingly does wrong: his wrong-doing is a matter of ignorance. He will not have this. He thinks it is fanciful and against the facts. Character much more than intelligence or knowledge is back of right living. Knowledge, unfortunately, is not a guarantee of morals. Choices are influenced by passion as much as by mind. So he adds to his prerequisites a good disposition. He was familiar with the sick, the unruly, and the distempered. History has it that he had Alexander the Great for a pupil. So he is a bit cautious about admitting that even his own handbook on ethics, sound as he takes it to be, is likely to turn a bad man into a good one. It is good for men of good disposition, and in such men lies the hope of society and of the city. On their effective willingness to take administration in their own hands depends the control of the forces of evil and disorder. They will have superior knowledge because they have superior dispositions, but this disposition was not the gift of their knowledge but the gift of nature. Politically they are a privileged class, not, however, for their own sake but for the city's. And the larger the city, the more democratic it is seen to be, the more the needs of the many will be the clamoring needs. Consequently politics is not a theory of the ideal city, but a practical administration of an actual city's affairs.

Given, then, the conditions of living well, what is the method of it? Aristotle's answer is, the controlled formation of habit. It is that discipline of natural propensities which keeps them from running to their extreme illustration. In the face of danger, for example, a man may be rash or run away. Nature attends to that. Men are naturally foolhardy or cowards. They need to cultivate that habit of meeting danger which we call courage. This is a blend of impulse and knowledge, which tends to keep a man steady in the face of danger. He cultivates this habit by keeping reflection active in cases of danger, finding out how he is inclined now to this extreme and now to that, and seeking a balance between these inclinations. This is, in illustration, the whole method of controlled habit formation. Out of it come those excellent things which we call the virtues. They, courage, temperance, liberality, and the rest, are the dignifying names we give to natural propensities transformed into habits of behavior through the exercise of reflection. It is by cultivating these habits that a man comes to live well, and comes to live supremely well when the conditions are favorable. Of all virtues, friendship is the best, for no one would choose to live without friends even if he had all other goods. (Book VIII)

Ethics is, then, the knowledge of that practice which mediates the passage from living to living well. Nature furnishes the material and art the method. There is also the theoretical side to the subject, for there is not only the practical interest in habit, there is also the theoretical interest in the good. Right and good are not quite the same sort of adjectives or nouns. Right has about it the flavor of method and administration. It is a matter of adjustments, so that when we think of right alone, it is justice that shines as the most brilliant of the virtues. It is the great concern of courts and cities. It is keeping the balance between conflicting claims and requires much knowledge and computation. The good, however, is something desired, or something treasured, or something aimed at. It is not a matter of practical determination but of theoretical definition, as is clear enough even from the popular conception of the good as that at which one aims, and from the proverbial expression of "hitting or missing the mark." There is uncertainty, however, as to just what the good is, and there are conflicting theories about it. A definition is needed.

Since the good is a possession, it may readily be confused with possessions. But any theory tainted with this confusion is unsound. Possessions are, in some sense or other, all goods. The good in the plural, goods, that is, is a name for them. And it is an easy theory which seeks *the* good by trying to find out what all goods have in common. This, in general, is an easy kind of theory, but it is usually quite superficial, for a common character found must be carried over into nature if it is to have any theoretical value. Man, for example, is not some quality which all men have in common; it is rather what-it-is-to-be-a-man, and this carries us straight to the operations of nature. Now it is clear enough that pleasure or the promotion of pleasure is a common quality associated with goods. They bring pleasure and they promote pleasure. It is claimed therefore that the good is pleasure or the pleasant. Aristotle subjects this theory to an analysis which has stood well the test of time. We do little beyond repeating him. He observes that the distinction between pleasure and the pleasant is important. For pleasure divorced from that which is pleasant becomes something very vague and indeterminate. There may be those who are satisfied with pleasure, no matter how it comes. They are not, however, people who are generally looked upon as good illustrations of possessors of the good. And not only that—and it may be dismissed as having no more value than appeal to popular estimation—not only that, but the pursuit of pleasure as pleasure is demonstrably self-destructive. It destroys a man. It shortens his life, cuts him off from friends and society, fills him with disease, and nauseates him in the end. This can hardly be called the good or that at which a man's life aims. The popular distrust and suspicion of the pursuit of pleasure is thoroughly well-grounded. It is different with the pleasant. Even confirmed hedonists—the pleasure men—confirm this, for they recommend discrimination, prudence, and even wisdom in the choice of pleasures. Better to be Socrates dissatisfied than a pig satisfied, said John Stuart Mill centuries later, condensing pages of argument into a telling epigram. It is better. So the theory of pleasure must be turned into a theory of the pleasant.

But this, thinks Aristotle, is the complete abandonment of the hedonistic theory. The moment we turn to the pleasant as distinct from pleasure, we find that every free and unimpeded natural activity is pleasant, and that the matter of being more or less pleasant is a matter of each of them in its own terms, and not a matter of them in sum or in relation to each other. Walking may be more or less pleasant, and so may riding be, but you cannot have a double pleasure by walking and riding at once. Nor can you say strictly that it is a greater pleasure to ride than to walk. It may be, but that depends on circumstances. Clearly, when you want the pleasure of walking, it is not a greater pleasure to ride. We never want interruptions in wanted pleasure, if that can be avoided. Furthermore, there is an obvious relativity in the pleasant, and even in the good. Old Heraclitus would say that salt water was a good drink for fishes but a bad drink for men. The good may be, and indeed is, the pleasant, but it is the pleasant in connection with characteristic activity. We are forced to recognize the good of a plant, of an animal, and of a man. For men, the good is the pleasant—if one still wants pleasure—but the pleasant in connection with that activity which characterizes and distinguishes man.

This is his life of reason. The theoretical life is the good life, the best life; and the theoretical man is the good man, the best man. We should be stupid to be deceived by the words. We should remember what the life of reason is and implies.

Then we can see Aristotle's picture of the theoretical man in
the proper light. We can then see why he said of it in one of
those passages in which he lets the beauty of the Greek
language have its way: "If reason is divine compared with
man, then the life of reason is divine compared with man's
mortal life. There is no need to follow those who advise a
man, because he is a man, to think about that, or a mortal,
because he is mortal, to think about that. For each man, as
far as it is possible, should not *die,* but should make everything contribute to a life true to the highest that is in him.
Although this is small in size, in power and dignity, it sur-
passes all the rest." (477b 30)

I began this lecture with a reference to Santayana's book
and with that reference I may close. He says that with
Aristotle "everything ideal has a natural basis, and everything
natural an ideal development." He says this of Aristotle's
conception of human nature. But it must be said also of his
conception of nature at large. The history of the soul must
not be forgotten. It is one with the history of nature, and
different from nature only as one illustration of the development of nature is different from another. And the *Physics*
and *Metaphysics,* culminating in a theology, ought not to be
forgotten. On that first mover who does not move with a
push, but whose presence awakens desire, everything in
heaven and earth depends—everything. So each thing is
drawn to seek its good, to be what it might be, to realize its
powers, to find no hindrances except the inertia of matter and
the incidents of chance, and so turn the possible into those
numberless illustrations of the actual which diversify existence.

Man is only the supreme illustration. The stone turned into a doorstep can illustrate it also. Man is supreme only because in him there is realized the power to say that all this is what nature is. He has the last word which is the discovery of the first.

*The Philosopher at Work:*
*Preliminary Reflections*

# Preliminaries I:
## Remarks, with a Note on the Logic

The writings attributed to Aristotle present a difficult problem to the biographer and the historian. It is also a fascinating problem. I shall not, however, deal with it in these lectures. These writings, whoever their author may have been, whatever may have been the reasons for writing them, and whatever social or educational situations they may represent, make up a document which provides intellectual stimulation and excitement. They would, I think, do that today, were they now discovered for the first time and discovered in total ignorance of their author or their history. Were they rewritten today with the same intellectual temper which characterizes them but with our present factual knowledge as their basis, they would, I am sure, command the greatest attention and respect. They represent both a manner of engaging in the enterprise of learning and a body of information on a great variety of subjects. So far as the information is concerned, the reader is often amazed at its extent, its accuracy, its detail and its penetration. If he looks at it with the eyes of an historian, he is astonished to find repeatedly that Aristotle knew centuries ago much that we have only recently discovered by diligent inquiry, and regard as new. But the reader will also find much that is very bad misinformation. He is sure to be perplexed by the mixture and wonder how it could be possible that a man who could observe so well could often observe so ill. But the reader will find, I am sure, that even when the information is misinformation, the knowledge not knowledge at all, the manner of dealing with it and the spirit of inquiry brought to bear on it are impressive. Aristotle has repeatedly been found to have something to say about nature, life, soul, and man which is provocative. It is this fact which gives me the general theme of these lectures.

I have referred to the biographical and historical problem set by the writing, not simply to dismiss it. There is good reason to remember it. To set forth with conviction the opinions of Aristotle implies some confidence with regard to him and his age. It implies some confidence with regard to what we call his school, the Lyceum, and its activities. It implies some confidence with regard to the writings, which of them he wrote and which not, whether he wrote any of them at all, what they were written for, and what their historical fate has been. Personally, I have very little confidence about these matters. Perhaps, however, I ought to say that the more I have studied them, the less confident I become in making the results of the study a framework in which to set him and his activities. For example, we are told on as good authority as we have that he entered Plato's school, the Academy, at the age of seventeen and remained there twenty years, until Plato died. It is consequently natural to see in Aristotle an outcome of Plato's teaching, in sympathy or out of sympathy with it, and to begin consideration of him with a consideration of his relation to his master. I find this method more difficult than helpful. Approaching Aristotle's relation to Plato from the point of view of Plato's writings, and approaching it from the point of view of Aristotle's writings, involves me in questions more perplexing than illuminating. From Plato's writings I get little suggestion of the prime sources and inspiration of Aristotle and from Aristotle's writings I get a rendering of Plato which I find well-nigh impossible when I read what Plato wrote. I get more and more curious about the relation between the two men, but I find it better, in reading Aristotle, to put the curiosity aside, and read him as if Plato were unknown to me except for what I find Aristotle saying about him. This position is, however, often embarrassing.

I might have used other illustrations to indicate the consequences which arise from my neglect of biography and history. Without conviction as to what Aristotle did and did not write, there can be little conviction as to what he said and did not say. Yet I am forced to speak, as I have usually done, of Aristotle as having something to say about nature, life, soul, and man. Did he say what I shall say he said? I think he did, or, at least, something very much like it. The impression I have received of him as a mind from the writings attributed to him is, I believe, justified by the writings, but I am very conscious of the fact that I may often have read, as we say, into them some things that are not there. Yet I must say this in defense. If I have done this historically improper thing, I must put the blame not on myself but on the writings. I am conscious of their compulsion as distinct from my own intent. They have altered my ways of thinking, as distinct from confusing them. I recognize in them the source of ideas that I never brought to bear on them. I am constantly excited by sentences neglected in former readings, which sentences throw clearer and sometimes altered light on what I have read before. Now all this leads me to believe that if what I shall say was not said by Aristotle, it is said in the Aristotelian spirit and method. But I must admit some enthusiasm for a source from which I have derived much.

There is one other preliminary which should be noted. Among the historical consequences of the writings which I shall now and hereafter call the writing of Aristotle, or Aristotle for short, is the formation of what might be called a philosophical vocabulary. That vocabulary went from Greek into Latin, and from both Greek and Latin into our modern languages, and for us into English. The result is a vocabulary whose current usage is often not the Aristotelian usage. So while it is natural and by far the easiest thing to do, to expound Aristotle in terms of this vocabulary, it is a very questionable thing to do.

Perhaps the most general and uniform impression which the writings of Aristotle make upon the reader is an impression of system and order. The information they contain covers a wide variety of subjects, but the information is ordered and at times tortured into a system of knowledge in which branches of knowledge are distinguished and related to each other. The whole body of knowledge, for example, is divided into the theoretical, the practical, the creative, and this division is based on three recognized attitudes of man, namely, the reflective or curious attitude, the moral and civic attitude, and the artistic or manipulating attitude. Man reflects on his existence in the world, he has to live with his friends and neighbors, his trials and successes, his fellow citizens and foreigners, and he makes things and writes poetry. Although these activities are those of a whole man and not of three distinct men held apart in one body, they can be distinguished and consequently give rise to books or treatises or discussions which set forth the procedures involved and the results reached when man acts in these ways. Hence we have the threefold division of knowledge. But we have more in the Aristotelian system. The procedures or writings involved in these divisions receive much attention. They receive so much that the study of the system as a whole seems to be derived from the attention paid to method. In the building up of the system logic seems to be more controlling and important than subject-matter. As a consequence of all this, the reader is naturally beguiled by the system and its coherence, and has his attention distracted from the manner in which it was built up. Clearly, however, the way the system was built up gives to the system whatever value it has as a rendering of the material with which it deals. The materials, as Aristotle dealt with them, produced the system, not the system the materials. Consequently I start, not with the division of knowledge and come down from there, but with the inquiry which Aristotle appears to regard as of first importance as a start, namely the psychology.

# Preliminaries II: Περὶ Ψυχῆς

## BOOK I, CHAPTER 1

I begin with Aristotle's book—or three books—on the soul, because of the way the book itself begins. In the opening sentence he says that the study of the soul deserves to be put in the first rank of all studies. Where I have used the word "study," he uses the word ἱστορίαν. His word goes naturally into our "history," for our word is the one he used transliterated. It is tempting to speak, therefore, of the "history of the soul." It has a happier sound than "psychology," and it is appropriate even if the Greek word ἱστορία with Aristotle meant something different from what "history" usually means with us. His word had itself an interesting history. The Greeks spoke of a man who was wise in city matters as a ἵστωρ, as a man who knows or is wise. But in order to become a ἵστωρ a man had to collect information about cities and

men, and so the Greeks made a verb from the noun to indicate this collecting of information. And then with their
wonted economy in the use of words they invented ἱστορία
as a name for the information collected. This is happily illustrated by Herodotus. He went about collecting information
about cities and men and put the results in a book with the
name *The History of Herodotus*. It was easy to transfer the
word to collections of information about anything, animals
and the soul, for example, as is illustrated by Aristotle's and
our own use—now a little antiquated—of "natural history."
With Aristotle the history of anything was a rather serious
and laborious business. So I have used the word "study."

I have said that it is appropriate to speak of the "history of
the soul." I mean appropriate in our sense of the word for, to
anticipate a little, with Aristotle the soul is something which
grows, which comes to be what it is, and so has a history in
that sense. It is a life, and so the student of it should exhibit
that life in its development. So we may say in general of
Aristotle's psychology that it comprises the information—or
part of it—which he collected about the soul, and the use of
this information to set forth what the life of the soul is like.

Having said something about the word ἱστορία, perhaps
I ought to say something about the word ψυχή or soul. The
Greeks themselves seemed to have been troubled a little about
it. They were not quite sure why they called the soul the
"soul." The indications are that the word ψυχή was the word
for "breath" before it was the word for "soul," and so could
mean that which appeared to leave a man's body when he
died. The departure of the soul was often pictured by the way

of the mouth, and imagination could represent the matter as something like a bird or butterfly leaving the mouth with wings set for flight to another place. (The "winged words" of Homer is another example.) Here we have a hint of the beginning of the tales which have to do with Cupid and Psyche. The flight of the soul seems to have been fixed in men's minds before ever they studied psychology. One may say that this was quite natural, indeed, that it is quite natural. For the soul seems to be just that which leaves a man when he dies and goes somewhere else. The man's body remains but the man is gone. So the soul as a tenant of the body is a rooted conception before speculation about the soul arises. And it is natural, consequently, that psychology should so often begin with this rooted conception. Aristotle begins this way in his history of the soul, as we shall soon see. But it may be said now that he ends with this conception put away. The soul becomes with him not at all like something which can enter and leave a body. It is well, perhaps, to be advised of this at the start, for the soul with Aristotle is just that which was conceived to enter and leave, only with him it did neither. With him it is the recognition of the difference between the living and the dead which is the recognition of the soul, but in this recognition he does not find the soul to be like a being which can go in or out of a house. In this matter, however, there is a difficulty at one point which we shall have to consider.

Thus it may be said that whatever difficulty the Greeks may have had about the word "soul" or ψυχή, there was no uncertainty about what one was considering when he considered the soul. In other words, it was perfectly definite subject-matter to be studied. Everybody knew what you were talking about when you talked about it. Now it is often said that modern psychology has rid itself of the soul. Whether this is so or not I leave unconsidered. I refer to the impression in order to have our minds clear on the Greek—and I may add—our own unsophisticated attitudes in the matter. There is a very obvious difference between a living man and a dead one. This difference is summed up by saying that the former has a soul but the latter not. The former is body *and* soul, the latter body alone. We cannot obliterate this distinction. And it is this distinction which has had more to do with our thinking and living than any other that can be named.

So I come back to Aristotle's contention that the history of the soul is to be put in the first rank of studies. He says explicitly that if we consider all studies from the point of view of the discipline involved or that of the excellence and wonderfulness of their subject-matter, in both respects there is good reason for putting this study among the first. He says it is of great consequence in the matter of truth generally and particularly in the matter of truth about nature. He says that the soul is, as it were, the start of things that live. Many a modern will probably agree with him. There is a current tendency to make psychology pretty fundamental to all other intellectual interests. Whatever may be said of this, the judgment of Aristotle seems still to be good. An attempt to understand the soul may carry one pretty far, perhaps farther than the attempt to understand anything else.

Perhaps I ought to add here that the opening sentences of

the περὶ ψυχῆς raise or may raise expectations which the book does not fully meet. Why this is so will, I hope, appear as we go on. It may be said that to meet these expectations at all adequately involves the writing of many books.

"πάντῃ δὲ πάντως ἐστί τῶν χαλεπωτάτων λαβεῖν τινὰ πίστιν περὶ αὐτῆς." [1] I suppose that this means that Aristotle found the history of the soul to be in a very confused state. There was a good deal of uncertainty about the soul. He enumerates uncertainties, and one may conclude that the chief uncertainties were about what the soul *is* and about the way it should be examined. A study of these uncertainties in the light of what he does himself in his own account of the soul indicates that in his opinion the student had better not begin with them. These uncertainties are things to be bothered about only after one has done something else. They are not things to begin with. Here I may take the opportunity to point out one of the characteristics of Aristotle's method of inquiry. Obviously what I have now to say is not derived from the psychology alone. Nor can I claim that it is definitely formulated by Aristotle. It is rather something which one discovers as characteristic of the man's temper of mind.

I take a specific example. One of the chief uncertainties about the soul is bound up with the question: What is it? Well, what is it? The question is worth attention before we attempt to answer it. What is it that we want to know when we want to know what the soul is? A little attention ought to convince us that we must know what the soul is to begin with. In other words, if we do not know what we are talking

---

[1] "To reach some conviction about it [the soul] is one of the most difficult things of all in every respect." *De Anima* I, ch. 1.

about when we talk about the soul, there is no sense in talking about it. That is, if we ask what the soul is and are at the same time uncertain whether there is a soul, it is not very clear what we are talking about. So if we do not know what the soul is, there is little use in asking what it is. As Aristotle says, we must always begin with what we know if we want to get on. And by this I think he clearly meant that no inquiry can produce its own subject-matter. To put the matter in another way—the inquiry situation cannot be antedated, and in that situation, subject-matter and inquiry into it are there to begin with. His psychology as a whole may be considered as a demonstration of that fact, and I shall try to show later that he has packed it all into a single sentence. Just now I should like to comment on the matter.

I begin with an experience. Once in considering knowledge, I asked how would a man go to work if he wanted to find out something about frogs. A naive student said he would collect a number of frogs. A clever student asked: How does he know that it is frogs he is collecting? I can see how the naive student might find out something about frogs, but I do not see how the clever student ever could.

So with regard to the soul: we must first have a soul. So in general: to have inquiry, we must first have subject-matter. To have perception, we must first have something perceived, to have memory, we must first have something remembered, to have feeling, we must first have something felt, to have thought, we must first have something thought of. In general, to have inquiry we must first have something inquired into. Any other start is futile.

Let us try another start, that of John Locke, for example.

Let us take other illustrations—life, morality, art, religion.

From all these illustrations, it becomes clear, that we can begin only where we do begin. Now it is characteristic of Aristotle that he takes this fact seriously. Instead of taking it as an obvious fact to be forgotten, he takes it as an important fact never to be forgotten—a fact or the fact basic to any confident theory of things.

Return now to the soul. We may now say that if the question, What is the Soul? has a meaningful answer, it must be derived from the situation in which the question does not imply uncertainty as to what the soul is. What the soul *is* is an illustration of *what* it is; or *what* it is, is an illustration of what it *is*. It is this difference of emphasis which defines a problem. In other words, What is the Soul? It is a question with a meaning only as an emphasis can fall either on *what* or *is,* and to get this variation in emphasis there must first be a situation from which the emphasis is absent.

## REMAINING CHAPTERS OF BOOK I

After enumerating in chapter I questions and difficulties about the soul, Aristotle proceeds in the remaining chapters of the book to give an account of the opinions of his predecessors and contemporaries. This account I shall not examine in detail for its historical interest. I may comment on its outcome and effect.

He observes, as already noted, that it is the difference between the living and the dead (ἔμψυχος, ἄψυχος: souled and unsouled) which identifies the soul. He finds that this differ-

ence has been condensed into two chief particulars: κινήσει
καὶ τῷ αἰσθάνεσθαι. These Greek words are usually translated as "motion" and "perception," and we can probably do
no better. The living and the dead differ in the way they
move, and in the fact that the living perceive, and the soul is
invoked to account for this difference.

In the first place, it is to be noted that these two particulars
identify the difference and are so far just the soul. It is by a
certain kind of movement (moving in a certain way), and
by perceiving, that the living are or have souls as distinct
from the dead. To invoke the soul to explain them may be
natural, but it looks a little suspicious—a little like invoking
the roundness of a circle to explain the circle's difference from
a square, or the sweetness of sugar to explain sugar's difference from salt.

But we should first examine the difference, that is, why the
general difference is reduced to these two particulars. First as
to motion: the Greek word is κίνησις. It's a little troublesome
when we translate it into "motion," for although we say it
means what we mean by motion, it also meant much more.

"Action" might be better, but it is not usual. Etymologists
suggest that the root comes from a verb meaning "to go,"
and that is not so bad, for it suggests that one of the prime
differences between the living and the dead lies in the way
they go. Both may be said to go from here to there, in straight
or curved lines, from hot to cold, from hard to soft, from wet
to dry; but the living alone go from seed to fruit, from genes
to organism, from youth to age, from a boy to a man, from
a man to a general, from fear to courage, from peace to war,

from good to bad, etc. Furthermore, in these their peculiar goings, the motivation or the beginning or start of the goings seem to be inside instead of outside. In the other sort of goings, the start seems to be outside. Now all these sorts of goings are covered by that Greek noun κίνησις and the Greek verb κινεῖν, which we translate "a motion" and "to move." I may remark that we still have the Greek usage in our own term, when we use such expressions as "make a motion," "the peace movement," "emotion," "commotion," etc. Aristotle seems to have reduced, or to have found reduced, all these various kinds of motion to two basal sorts, "motion starting within," and "motion starting without," those motions starting within the body or thing moved and those starting without. I try to express it as simply as possible, because elaborate words are often bad, such as "spontaneous." To have a soul, therefore, is to go in such a way that the motions are prompted in their character from within rather than from without.

An acute mind might here suspect a difficulty. Dead things or at least things said to be dead, like gunpowder, ought to have a soul. (The instance of Thales [2] for instance. Here make a comment on φύσις and the consequent limitations of motions that are not "natural." The "natural" motions seem to be the kind that raise problems but the not-natural seem too evident and simple to raise much of a problem.)

Secondly, as to perception: the Greek word is αἰσθάνεσθαι. Aristotle uses it in the infinitive form—*perceiving* rather than *perception*. This is important, for the emphasis is to fall on an act instead of upon a faculty. From the word we get the

[2] See p. 31. *De Anima* I, ch. 2, 405a 19–21.

word "aesthetics." In the Greek the word has a special and a general meaning. In its special or more restricted sense it covered such acts as "seeing," and "hearing," etc. Indeed, it is supposed by some to have meant originally to "hear." This is interesting as a reminiscence of the spoken word. The restricted usage is "sensing." In its general meaning it included such acts as remembering and thinking, was indeed a term for what we call mental operations, involving the soul to explain perception.

Perception as a "taking through" or "in."

The soul's vocabulary is an interesting vocabulary.

I am tempted to digress from Aristotle and make some remarks relative to the situation generally, or rather as it involves man.

THINKING OF DEATHLESS THINGS

1. I note again that it is the distinction between the living and the dead that identifies the soul. If we did not die we should probably never talk of the soul at all. The gods do not have souls. Or they do not have them as we have them, for the gods, although their experiences are often much like ours, do not die. One may say, although it is a little confusing, that their souls are their bodies. It is hard for us to think of them clearly, because we are always bothered by the consideration that they live and so must have bodies, but they do not die, and so cannot have bodies. One thing is clear: they are never interested in their own psychology, it gives them no problems. They are interested only in human psychology.

It is quite unorthodox to think that the dead, or that which does not die, have souls, although one might here remember Thales whom Aristotle mentions. Yet we are told we ought not to think in this way. Oxygen has no soul, electricity has none, matter has none. A dead or lifeless universe is a soulless universe. Thales, however, is evidence that this way of thinking was not always orthodox. Nor is it by any manner of means dead. It persists in spite of us. We may not use the word "soul," but we do use the word "power." (Develop "power.") Water *seeks* its level, there is attraction and repulsion, nature *does* this and that. (This would be behavior.) Matter has no soul, we say, and yet we say it is deathless, and yet it operates. It has power to do what it does. It is just like the gods, not interested in its own psychology, interested in ours enough to produce it. All this is ample evidence that without death there would be no interest in psychology at all, or perhaps it would be better to say that interest in psychology would be precisely like interest in chemistry or physics or living. It would be indeed interest in what we do by the exercise of our powers, just as the ways of the gods and matter are that.

2. Let us then forget death for a little while. Then it becomes evident that it is we ourselves who do what we do. All the mystery of the soul is gone. The ample proof of this is the fact that there is no mystery about the soul in anything that is immortal. I say again, it now becomes we that do what we do, and by "we" I mean our bodies when they are exempt from death. It is our eyes that see and our brains that think— but all this quite free from any distinction between soul and

body, life and death, precisely as it is oxygen that burns, irrespective of any distinction between oxygen's body and oxygen's soul, between oxygen's life and its death. The only distinction is now that between a thing and what it does. We should have a situation which a being with a soul would call materialistic, but which a being without a soul would not, could not, in fact.

3. That there is no interest in the soul in the case of anything untouched by death, but only an interest in what the thing does, is itself interesting. It is so interesting that I could talk about it for the rest of the session. No wonder Aristotle put psychology first among studies! But before I return to him, I would say this:

(*a*) It is, finally, most important in thinking, to begin with what identifiable things do, to analyze them, dissect them, if you will, in order to find out how what they do is connected with their make-up, and what their doing in connection with their make-up effects and implies. I would make this concrete for the study of man by example.

A man sometimes weeps. Now how is his weeping connected with his make-up? We get the lacrymose glands. Without them he could not weep. So we can say that weeping is a consequence of the stimulation of the lacrymose glands. There doesn't seem to be any doubt of this whatever. Now what is a consequence of a man's weeping, or what happens to a man when he weeps? The answer is simple, he is sorry. So far, all seems to be perfectly definite and clear. But now the situation has become interesting and exciting. Instead of being at the end of the matter, we seem to be just at the beginning of

what impresses as really important. Just the weeping is not
very important—that is, the weeping without the sorrow. The
glands are not very important; anything else would do as well
provided the stimulation of it made a man weep. If stepping
on his toe without his having any glands at all was what
made him weep, we should be just as satisfied with that as
we are with glands. But the man—whether toe or glands—is
sorry! So we ask: why does the stimulation of the glands
make him sorry? His make-up and the stimulation of his
glands do not answer that question, cannot answer it. The
man's sorrow is humanly the only important matter. We may
admit a great deal of intellectual satisfaction in finding out
that crying is a natural consequence of the stimulation of the
glands, and also that sorrow is equally a natural consequence,
but it is hard to conceive this satisfaction apart from interest
in sorrow as sorrow and the desire to do something about
sorrow.

(b) Without going any farther at this point, one thing
seems perfectly clear, namely, that it is not our make-up, our
glands, the stimulation of them or weeping, that makes the
situation humanly interesting, but sorrow alone. And this
illustration can be generalized. It is difficult, I find, to state it
satisfactorily, in generalized form, because of ambiguities in
language. We might use the illustration to help us and say:
It is not the fact of things like bodily make-up, nor the fact of
stimulation, that makes the world interesting to us, but the
fact of things like sorrow. To get a happy word to cover
things like bodily make-up and stimulation, and a happy
word for things like sorrow, is not easy. It is not the quantita-

tive, but the qualitative; it is not the mechanical, but the teleological; it is not the body, but the soul; it is not matter, but mind, etc. It is not what things are, nor the way they behave, but what they effect. It is not existence, but the consequence of existing. I rather like this last. We might say that the soul is interesting because it is not *an* existence, but a consequence of existing. But that the soul should be a consequence of existence may be important in trying to answer the question: What existence *is?* What must we say about existence if a man can be sorry?

This brings me back to Aristotle. The root trouble he finds with his predecessors and contemporaries is that they regard the soul as an existence instead of a consequence of existing, when they invoke it to explain motion and perception. It is right to link motion and perception with the soul, but wrong to do it as they did it. They recognize the distinction, but misconstrue it.

## BOOK II

This brings me to Book II and Aristotle's own definition of the soul: ἐντελέχεια ἡ πρώτη σώματος φυσικοῦ ὀργανικοῦ, "the first entelechy of a natural organic body." (Hammond tr.) That is about as intelligible in Greek as it is in English, for it is not difficult to see that ἐντελέχεια equals "entelechy," and πρώτη equals "first," and σώματος equals "body," and φυσικοῦ equals "physical," and ὀργανικοῦ equals "organic."

I might proceed to expound these words. The definition may be said to be a very happy and exact one, if one under-

stands Aristotle's vocabulary. If one does not, it is quite meaningless in the English translation. We may begin with "body,"
for that is easy. But the body must be "physical." This means
it must have an inside motion or a motion internally prompted
as to its character or kind. But this "physical body" must be
"organic." This means that it must have organs, instruments,
tools, glands connected with these movements. Now we come
to "entelechy." Literally, the Greek word cannot go into a
single English word. Even in Greek, although written in our
texts as one word, it is a compound of three, like "not-
withstanding." It is clear proof that Aristotle had linguistic
troubles of his own. This word is almost exclusively his. Apparently he coined it. The three Greek words are ἐν = in,
τέλος = end, ἐχεῖν = to have. So "to-have in the end," the
"to have-at-last," what is had at last.[3] "First" evidently means
first. So the soul = the first what-is-had-at-last of, etc. This is
not as bad as it looks. For take a body—this pencil—and follow
it along. It is at last a writing body. To be a writing body is
its "entelechy," but to be that it must have first the power to
write, and this, its "first entelechy," is this power as it evinces
itself. We can now phrase this differently; the "first entelechy"
of a physical organic body is that which distinguishes it from
other such bodies. Plants, animals, and men are distinguished
as such by their "entelechies" or their souls. Or to go back to
my humble illustration, a pencil is distinguished from a pen
as lead is from ink. Or we may speak of a lead pencil and an
ink pencil, but must remember here that a pencil is a natural
organic body.

[3] But see p. 36, footnote 1.

To return to Aristotle, and to his predecessors, restating their error: We may now say that they, like him, distinguished soul and body and identified the distinction in the same way. In going on from this point in an attempt to define the soul, they raised the question of the relation of the soul to the body. Now Aristotle's criticism is that they brought to bear upon this question types of relation which are inappropriate.[4] He cites principally three: 1) the soul is related to the body as two bodies are related to each other; 2) as harmony is related to an instrument; 3) as number is related to what is numbered. Over against these he puts his own: the soul is related to the body as what a thing does to the thing that does it. Like his illustration of the ax and the eye. εἰ γὰρ ἦν ὁ ὀφθαλμὸς ζῷον, ψυχὴ ἂν ἦν αὐτοῦ ἡ ὄψις. (*De Anima* II, ch. 1) This latter illustration could hardly be bettered.

It is of first importance that we get this conception of the relation between soul and body in terms of the illustrations, before we try to get it in terms of the Aristotelian terminology. That terminology identifies nothing to begin with. It involves an elaboration of what is first identified. This must be noted as characteristic of Aristotle's method of inquiry. I want to make this definite. Having identified the soul and its relation to the body, he asks at once one of the questions raised in Book I: Is the soul separable or inseparable, independent or dependent, an element entering into a composite or not?

___

[4] In the margin of the manuscript studies is written at this point: "This should be put differently for the time being. Predecessors dealt with motion and perception in terms of a wrong interpretation of the relation between soul and body."

Now this question implies a number of general ideas to which one may be led and in terms of which one may build up a system; but one cannot begin with the system. There are categories, but one mustn't begin with them: one arrives at them, and having arrived at them one can ask whether the soul belongs to one rather than the other; but to answer one must proceed from the soul to the category, not from the category to the soul. Now Aristotle's own answer to the question is obvious: the soul is not separable. He modifies this later as we shall see.

I digress again.[5] What must we say about existence if a man can be sorry? But now I am going to change the question because of Aristotle's illustration of vision as the soul of the eye. This illustration can be worked out in the same way as the other. A man sees as well as weeps. His seeing is connected with his bodily make-up by means of the eye. When his eye is stimulated he sees. But what does he see? The answer is clear, a world about him; or better, he sees his body, and about his body a horizon containing a great variety of shapes and colors requiring a rather elaborate vocabulary to describe. For short, we may say he sees a visible world, and we say visible (or "seeable") because he sometimes sees and sometimes not. In other words, seeing is an event in his life, and an event which reveals a world or an existence which his body occupies. Seeing is a consequence of his existing, and ought to throw light on existence. Now what light does it throw? The answer is obvious: existence is something that can become visible. This is not silly; at least Aristotle does

[5] In the margin occurs the note: "Explain what I mean by 'digress.'"

not seem to think it is. It is not silly, because it leads to the question, what are the conditions of visibility? Now it will not do at all in trying to answer this question to point to the man, his eyes, their stimulation and the fact that he sees, for the very simple reason that it is only in a visible world that these things can be pointed to. In other words, one must *start* with the visible world, if the conditions of visibility are to be explored.

Before continuing the digression, I want to remind you of certain details of Aristotle's history of the soul, growing out of his definition of what the soul is.

1. The definition, we may now say, grew out of his examination of attempts to understand the soul as a source of perception and motion in terms of the relation between soul and body.

2. His own view of that relation is that the body and soul are related as an instrument or organ and what the instrument or organ does are related, when this relation is identified in the case of living things. He defines the soul accordingly.

3. Now this definition of his involved the recognition that everything that lives has a soul, plants and animals as well as men. The soul is coextensive with life, and the difference, such as there is, between life and soul is just the difference between life at large and plant life, animal life and human life. That is, whatever can be said about living plants, animals, and men, irrespective of the fact that they are plants, animals, and men, is said about life. Everything else is said about the soul. The soul is then what is recognized in recognizing different kinds of life.

4. On this basis Aristotle proceeds to indicate the differences between different kinds of soul:

(*a*) Plant: nutrition and reproduction.

(*b*) Animal: (*a*) plus sensation, memory, imagination, experience.

(*c*) Human: (*b*) plus reason or thought.

All have natural motion and growth, and all have appetite or desire in some degree.

5. Now if we think of the soul in terms of these distinctions, we observe that (*c*) implies (*b*) and (*a*), and (*b*) implies (*a*), but (*a*) does not imply (*b*) or (*c*) nor does (*b*) imply (*c*). That is, soul as displayed in life at large presents a growth or development from (*a*) to (*c*). The "parts" of the soul are to be understood not as detached parts that are put together, but as just these recognizable distinctions in the development.

6. This same development idea is carried out in detail. As for example: in sensation we have touch, taste, smell, hearing, sight. The latter implies the earlier, but not the earlier the later. Again, sensation, perception, experience, understanding, reason. It is this development idea which makes the expression "history of the soul" appropriate in our sense of "history."

7. Now this may be stated in the Aristotelian terminology. Since a plant, for instance, can do what it does do, it may be said to have the *ability* or *power* to do what it does do. Hence δύναμις, "potentiality," "faculty." Since, however, the power to do something is not the same as doing it, the doing of it is something actual as distinct from potential, and we have

ἐνέργεια or "actuality." And since the actuality as actually effected, the working as actually worked, is somewhat different from just the working, we have ἐντελέχεια or "realization." Hence the soul is "the first realization of a natural organic body."

8. Hence the soul as a natural fact or fact of nature is to be regarded as the passage from δύναμις to ἐνέργεια to ἐντελέχεια. These Greek words are just as good as the English "potentiality," "actuality," and "realization," and vice versa, if one understands them in terms of the way they come to be used.

9. Now all the problems of the soul, or, more specially, the two problems of perception and motion, are to be stated according to Aristotle in terms of the definition of the soul as now formed. Each problem involves the analysis of a passage from δύναμις to ἐνέργεια to ἐντελέχεια—from "can work" to "working" to "work done."

10. Aristotle pays some attention to the lower orders of the soul, but his chief interest is in perception and motion, as these are carried as far as they can be. The details are not as important as the problem. The latter commits Aristotle to a wholly dynamic psychology. To work this out he used the materials he had.

Now it looks as if we should have to repeat the lines of thought we followed when we talked of the everliving or the gods. Suppose, for example, that we always saw without any interruption whatever. This is of course a supposition contrary to fact, but it does suggest that it is the fact that seeing is or may be interrupted, that turns vision into a problem.

Now one thing is quite clear, the field of vision is a field of inquiry. It is a field to be explored. What can be said about it?

1. It is an actual or factual or existing field. We ask a host of questions about it, and answer these questions by direct appeal to the field itself. In the field, for example, are many distinguishable bodies. We may explore their relations to one another. There are colors; there is light and shadow. All these we can explore without raising the question of the relation of the field of vision to anything not in that field. This is important.

2. The field is a whole and continuous. There are no gaps in it. It is limited only by the things in it—as this room by its walls. Beyond the field of vision is thus a little troublesome to deal with, for "beyond" seems to imply something which limits the field and is thus in some sense visible. Enlarging one's horizon: instruments and movement. The universe.

3. The effect of closing the eyes. Light and darkness. Closing the eyes leaves one in darkness. But darkness is hardly the absence of vision. It is rather the absence of things seen. Besides, darkness is not absent from the visible world. There are dark places in it, and it can be dark when the eyes are open.

4. The eyes, therefore, would seem to be not the condition of visibility, but rather the organ of seeing what is visible. Perception without eyes is difficult to imagine. The nearest we can come to it, is to note that the other senses do not give us the distinction between light and darkness. There is a

vast difference between being blind, in the sense of living always in the dark, and being blind, in the sense of living without the dark at all.

5. We seem, therefore, compelled to construe the conditions of visibility independent of the eyes. We seem forced back on the visible world itself. In this world it may be said that the distinction between light and darkness exists. We get the distinction either by closing our eyes or being, with them open, in the dark. We *see,* however, only the dark, and in this sense the dark is positive (as against where the dark is negative). We do not see the light, but see areas with their shapes instead. There are many experiments which make this clear. A cone of light in a dark room cannot be seen if the cone of light is all that we have. Within the field of vision we can distinguish the lighted parts from the dark, but we cannot distinguish between the field and anything beyond it. This fact deserves more attention than is often given to it. At the limits of vision, that is, there is no distinction between light and darkness. The limits are fixed by seeing lighted things.

6. Now the nearest we come to seeing light—or rather, we come to speak of light, as a consequence of two principle observations: (*a*) we see sources of illumination, and (*b*) we distinguish transparent media. Putting other things between the source and the thing illuminated, we observe that shadows are cast in varying degrees of darkness. When the shadow is at a maximum, the illumination of the object disappears. As the shadow approaches a minimum, the thing

that cast it approaches disappearance. The color of the transparent is thus the nearest we come to seeing light, or rather is what we mean by seeing light.

7. Now we seem to have come upon the conditions of visibility. We must have (*a*) a source of illumination; Aristotle calls this "fire," and that is well enough, as we can discover by striking a match in the dark. (*b*) We must have "the transparent," what Aristotle calls the διαφανές. And (*c*) we must have what he calls the το ἐπί of things, or a surface texture which when illuminated gives us color. When these conditions are operative, we have a visible world, a world which can be seen. When these conditions are not operative, nothing whatever can be seen. We could not affirm even that there was a dark world.

8. Here we might interject a popular discussion. We often ask, what does the world look like when it is not seen? and when we try to answer, we are often driven to the conclusion that the question is either meaningless, or that what the world *looks* like is simply the consequence of our seeing it. In this sad predicament, it is much better to examine the condition of visibility than to invent astonishing theories. Having examined these, we may then ask, what would the world be like in the absence of these conditions? That is a more sensible question and has more intelligible answers. But among the answers will not be the answer—dark.

9. To return: When we close our eyes we illustrate the condition of visibility. Closing the eyes is like casting an inclusive shadow over the world. It is like putting an opaque body in the visible world and then casting a black shadow

over the whole horizon. Only, in this case the shadow is seen. Disregarding this fact for the moment, it is to be noted that every opaque body does precisely what the eyelids do. It casts a shadow. Now the problem of vision becomes somewhat simplified in its statement, or it may be stated as follows. Given a being who can see the shadow cast when his eyelids are closed, how does he see what he sees when his eyes are open?

10. We should have this problem clearly before us in its statement. We must remember first of all that a man does see and can see. It is just this combination of "does" and "can" in him which is his soul. About this combination in him and that it is in him, there is no doubt. And it is in him, not after the manner in which water is in a pail. In this connection the only thing in him after that manner is his eyes, which cast a shadow when they are closed, but not when they are open. He cannot see without eyes, but if he could not see with them, all the eyes in the world would not help him. The power of seeing may be taken away from him, but it can't be put into him from without. When once he is produced he has the power to see native in him. (Say something about this power or power generally.) The manner of his production is ascertainable apparently without limits. Just so far as we can reproduce the condition of his natural genesis we reproduce him, but his natural genesis occurs long before we study it. And in so far as we study it, we never at any point whatever, put a power in him. His power is something mysterious and unnatural only when we have so conceived nature that a mystery or something not natural is required to account for

that power. If we do not conceive nature that way, then his power is not one whit different from the power of an ax to cut. The important things here we find are (*a*) that in order to exercise that power he must have eyes, or he receives that power through his eyes, and (*b*) there must be the conditions of visibility. His process of vision may be now defined as the effecting in him of the distinction between light and darkness, colors and shadows, and ultimately a shadow.

The key to Aristotle's theory of perception generally is found in what he rejects, namely in

1. The Empedoclean theory.
2. The Democritian theory.

We can touch with a stick as well as with the hand. The constant relation between things is what is perceived. Hence form and not matter in the soul. And so generally.

Omit examination of specific forms.

Go to the famous sentence: "As the forming form is to what is formed."

Correlation and conformity.

It may be said that Aristotle solves the problem of perception by a definition of what perception is. Perception is the conformity of the soul to what a man perceives, or to the conditions of perception. Now what does this amount to?

1. We may analyze the conditions of perception as much as we can or please, but the act of perception must always be added on, so to speak, to the analysis. It does not make the slightest difference where we locate the object of perception; there must be perception if the object is perceived. In general, the mechanism of perception is not perception.

2. We must now go back to the definition of the soul. If we ask for an *explanation* of perception, and mean by "explanation" the exhibition of how something is possible, then the soul is the only explanation of it. The soul, however, does not perceive itself; it perceives the object of perception. It is, therefore, what we call a power. It is at once the possibility and the act of perception. The soul in action, therefore, is the field of perception perceived (or realized as such a field. This is what is meant by "conformity"). It ought not to be surprising, therefore, that we see what is far away and also what is near, if in the field of perception there is "the far" and "the near." It ought not to be surprising that we perceive colors, if in the field there are colors. Thus perception is "in a sense" the things perceived, but "in a sense," the sense namely, which has already been indicated—the act of perception realized is the field of perception with this realization added. In terms of "consciousness," we may say that in the act of perception realized, there is no difference between "consciousness" and its objects, between a color and a color seen, or distance and distance perceived. It is only when the act is not realized that there can be such a distinction. Then the distinction is not between two fields, but between a field and a power which can act in conformity with that field. Aristotle's psychology is thus wholly free from presentative or representative theories of perception. It makes perception just like, in character, any other human activity, walking, digesting, breathing, etc. It is a useful exercise to try to deal with these other activities in the manner in which many psychologists have dealt with perception.

It is worth while pausing here to observe the psychology of
Aristotle in its historical perspective. The crucial matter here
is the different definitions of the soul. Aristotle's definition
linked the soul indissolubly with nature and the processes of
nature. Definitions later broke this linkage and left no room
for the soul in nature. As we pass from Aristotle to St. Augustine to Descartes,[6] to John Locke, and then to Immanuel
Kant, we have a progressive denaturalization of the soul, and
the exteriorization of nature as a separate and independent
realm of being. Consider the following quotations:

This is certain, that whatever alterations are made in the body, if
they reach not the mind, whatever impressions are made on the
outward parts, if they are not taken notice of within there is no
perception. Fire may burn our bodies with no other effect than it
does a billet, unless the motion be continued to the brain, and
there the sense of heat or the idea of pain, be produced in the
mind, wherein consist actual perception.[7]

There is no doubt at all that all our knowledge begins with experience; for how should our power to know be otherwise awakened to exercise, if this did not happen through objects which
affect our senses and partly of themselves produce presentations
(ideas) and partly set our understanding in motion to compare
them, unite them or separate them and so work over the raw
material of sense impressions into a knowledge of objects? [8]

[6] Woodbridge refers to A. A. Jascalevich, *Three Conceptions of the
Mind* (New York, 1926), a doctoral dissertation by one of his students
depicting this process of the denaturalization of mind, in Aristotle,
St. Augustine, and Descartes.

[7] John Locke, *An Essay concerning Human Understanding* (1690),
Book II, ch. 9, sec. 3.

[8] Immanuel Kant, *Critique of Pure Reason*, 2d ed., Introduction.

In both these instances we have clearly the denaturalization of the soul. The difference from Aristotle is enormous. The soul has become an independent entity which may think and feel and will (in Kant's three Critiques), but does so entirely in its own realm.

It is interesting to observe what nature has become in the two instances. With Locke, it has become the Newtonian system. With Kant it has become something very elusive: (*a*) The realm of objects which affect our senses and so far like Locke. (*b*) The great synthesis of the mind. (*c*) The unavailable correlate of this synthesis.

This denaturalized soul ruled almost unquestioned in psychology without much challenge except by the Neo-Scholastics down to the publication of William James's *Psychology* in 1890. Since then we have been in a muddle. Today we have behaviorism, which is in many respects like a return to Aristotle; but the return has not taken place through the study of him, but through the use of a similar method of approach and a study of animals as well as man.

I would not raise the question which of these views of perception and which of the definitions of the soul is correct. It is, however, interesting to point out that the later definition is like the one which preceded his own and was rejected by him. This is interesting as an historical event in the history of ideas.

I would point out also that the later definition produced a habit of mind and a problem which is alien to Aristotle. The habit of mind involved the impropriety of speaking of nature in human terms.

The problem was the problem of epistemology. I know no better or, perhaps, simpler statement of it than Locke gave.[9] The later definition posed this problem, and it has not yet been solved. See Montague's *Ways of Knowing* and Lovejoy's *The Revolt against Dualism.*[10]

CORRELATION AND CONFORMITY

One of the most significant sentences in the *Psychology* is the one already quoted: ὥσπερ τὸ αἰσθητικὸν πρὸς τὰ αἰσθητά, οὕτω τὸν νοῦν πρὸς τὰ νοητά.[11] There is a correlation between the powers of the soul and the fields of their operation. Perception is, as we have seen, an operation, exercise, or activity in a field of objects, just as seeing is the act of vision in a field of vision. There is no setting of the content of perception over against the field of perception, no setting of "states of consciousness" over against objects, no setting of the "psychical" over against the "physical" in any other sense than that which involves the act or operation of the "psychical" in the field of the "physical." Perception as a "psychical" act *is* perception of the "physical" world. What the physical world is like apart from or without perception is a question like the question, what it is like apart from or without any other operation. Now we may call this position of Aristotle "realism," or even "naive realism," but we should never forget

[9] Locke, *Essay,* Book IV, ch. iv; Fraser ed. (1896), II, 169.
[10] W. Pepperell Montague, *Ways of Knowing* (New York, 1925); Arthur O. Lovejoy, *The Revolt against Dualism* (La Salle, Ill., 1931).
[11] *De Anima* 429a 17; see discussion on pp. 45–47.

how inappropriate this is. For "realism" and "naive realism" in their usual acceptations are doctrines antithetical to a definition of the soul different from his, or they are antithetical to an approach to the problem of perception which neglects analysis of the conditions under which the problem is stated. The question whether we really perceive the physical world may be stated with little attention to what the soul is or what the physical world is. For example: We may *see* two moons when there *is* only one moon; how then can we *see* what *is?* Or we may debate the famous question of Sir William Hamilton, I think it was: "Ten men look at the moon; do they all see the same object?" Aristotle's analysis attempts to get back of these questions, and having done so, finds that the questions either have no meaning or are questions, not about perception, but about the physical world. For example: The fact that we sometimes see two moons and sometimes one is never explained by perception, but only by the fact that we have two eyes. The power to perceive can no more be taken out of nature than the power to move.

However difficult one may find Aristotle's exposition of all this in detail, the main position seems to be quite clear. In dealing with perception our attitude and our manner of approach and our procedure must not be one whit different from what they are when we deal with other operations, as for example, the operation of a magnet on iron filings or of acid on a photographic plate. As operations, the operation of vision, or in general, the operations of a man, are just like the operations of anything else, and his operations are just like theirs. In neither case is nature excluded. By first *defining* the soul and *defining* perception, he has made such exclusion, for himself at least, absurd and meaningless. Or: for him, when such an exclusion is made, everything else becomes absurd and meaningless.

It may, consequently, be said, I think, that the first result of his dealing with "the problem of perception" is to destroy the *problem*. There is no problem of *perception*: there is, however, a problem, or there are problems, of the things perceived. The second result—and it is of the greatest importance for his whole system—is to lead him to the quoted sentence. There is a correlation between powers and the fields of their exercise. This correlation involves always a field appropriate to the exercise of a given power. Nutrition, for example, is a power which is exercised in a field where there is food. If there were no food to eat, none would be eaten. If there were no place to move to, nothing would ever move to that place.

Now Aristotle follows this principle out and asserts that if there were no ideas, there never would be exercised the power of thought or reason. Ideas are not the products or creations of thought, they are rather the discoveries of thought. A man may find ideas as he may find a treasure in a field. For there is a field of ideas in nature fully as much as there is a field of food. If there is food for digestion, there is also food for thought. A man eats in a nutritious world, he perceives in a perceptual world, and he also thinks in an intellectual world. This last is no more in his head than the other two are. He may think *with* his head or his heart, just as he sees *with* his eyes, but there must be something to think about first. In all this matter Aristotle goes to the limit. Thinking is an operation or activity in an intelligible or intellectual world, and not an operation or activity imposed upon it. In the *Metaphysics* he says in a passage which Santayana has used to make a title for a book, ἡ γὰρ νοῦ ἐνέργεια ζωή, "for the exercise of reason is also life!" The word "life" here is not metaphorical. The soul *lives* in a realm of ideas as it *lives* in a realm of food. In terms of nature, we may say that things are just as much logically connected as they are connected in any other way. Socrates died from drinking poison, and he died in a world where "what-it-is-to-be-a-man" is logically connected with "what-it-is-to-be-mortal." Otherwise—and Aristotle goes as far as this—the poison would not have killed him. And, otherwise, too, the operations of thought could never lead to the control of nature. Knowledge would not be power and science would not be effective. Things could never be said to be what they are.

This doctrine of "realms of being," to use another phrase of Santayana's, which are correlative with the powers of the soul, so that we have a "realm of mind" correlative with the "life of reason," is fundamental to the soul's development. While the exercise of what we may call the higher powers of the soul involves the exercise of the lower, the higher neither grow out of the lower nor are imposed upon them. Nor is the unity of the soul an assemblage or synthesis of its powers. The soul develops, as we say, as a consequence of bodily organs, and this development in turn is a matter of natural history. The soul as the body's life or power is unitary from the start. Differentiation into powers is a consequence of the growth of organs. Under these restrictions, the development

of the soul may now be conceived as a movement from appetite to reason, or the movement of life from a world of food
to a world of ideas.

In this movement the exercise of the soul's powers results
in what may be called conformity. The soul's powers become
one with nature's, and the consequence is nature, but nature
limited by the body's location in it. This fact leads to a further
development of the doctrine of the soul to which I shall return later.

THE SOUL AS MOVER

We now turn to the second fundamental problem of the
soul, namely, the soul as a source or start of motion. We can
now guess that Aristotle deals with this problem somewhat
after the manner that he dealt with the problem of perception.
Obviously the soul does not move the body by pushing it
about. It is not quicksilver or anything like quicksilver. The
motions of the body are evidently, however, motions having
their *characteristic* source in the body. As we observe them
in operation they are like seekings of satisfactions or goods.
The powers of the soul are all in a sense appetitive powers,
they are exhibitions of desire, and desire, Aristotle finds, is
motivated by the objects of the desire. So far we have only a
variation of the doctrine of perception. Yet the variation is
important. It has much to do with Aristotle's general doctrine
of motion in the *Physics* and *Metaphysics*. Desire, simply
confronted with objects of desire, involves the release of
power. There is here a sort of inevitable working. It is all

sometimes summed up by speaking of the irrational soul and also of the passive reason. In general, desiderative movements are such that they may be called automatic.

There are also movements which may be called voluntary, movements which involve choice. Desires arise which are opposed and in conflict. Voluntary motions are those that follow upon the adjustment of this conflict. How then is this conflict adjusted?

Aristotle's answer is: through the operation of imagination and reason. A consequence of perception is imagination. Aristotle supports this by a number of interesting observations. There attends perception a kind of afterglow or afterimage. By the use of imagination, the soul changes the direction of its desires. It lives a calculating or prudential life. Imagination is thus found to be one internal source of motion.

Another source is reason.

Practical reason.

Theoretical reason.

# Preliminaries III:
## Features of Aristotle's Physics

Expositions of Aristotle are made difficult by the terms which are almost unavoidable. These terms are derived from him, but are seldom used as he used them. Yet they are the terms which it is natural to use, as "the physical," "the logical," "the natural."

The *Physics* of Aristotle is not opposed to modern physics in more than name. It is rather irrelevant. Practically none of the questions of modern physics are relevant to his; what is the velocity of sound? etc.

I. Subject-Matter. Here the insistence is that the proper subject-matter of physics is found in such illustrations as a seed becoming a plant, a child becoming a man, what is hot becoming cold, what is at rest becoming in motion, and (metaphorically) a stone becoming a doorstep. In general the subject-matter is the change from one state of affairs into another.

II. Assumption. Here the instance is that this change is a

change from what is to what can be or from what can be to what is, but not a change in the rearrangement of what is. It involves the distinction between the actual and the potential, and this distinction cannot be had in terms of the actual solely. When physical change is construed wholly in terms of the actual, no reason can be found why every change has not already occurred. In other words, construction in terms of the actual involves, upon analysis, a wholly static situation with no change possible in it. To get change something must be added on to the actual, but if this addition is something actual, the difficulty returns.

III. The *Physics* is thus an attempt to construe nature in dynamic terms as an exhibition of power. The formal statement of his general position is not difficult. The seat of power is matter, and matter is always actual. Power is not separate from matter, nor is it a force acting on matter or causing matter to act. It is simply what matter can be as distinct from what it now is. Only matter can act on matter, and this is accomplished by the impact of bodies. This impact is in effect the release of power. This release of power involves consequently endless or circular motion, that is, a continuous revolution of the cosmos. On cosmic revolution all other motions depend, and the consequent energizing of matter. Cosmic revolution, being the actualizing of the power to move, requires a first mover. Here, however, the cause of motion has to be of a different nature from a moving body. It moves by attraction rather than impact. It is logical rather than physical. The ultimate motivation of power is thus the logical condition implied by its exercise.

IV. The question may now be asked: how did Aristotle come to such a theory of nature, or such a physics? The answer seems to be twofold.

  1. Negatively, as a consequence of his analysis of the static conception of space, time, infinity, and motion.
  2. Positively, as a consequence of his psychology.

V. This leads to certain observations:

  1. His analysis of the static view seems still to be relevant to modern physics. As mathematics modern physics has no need of power, etc., but any connection of mathematics with the operation of motion involves physical realities which are not mathematical. Actual physical change is lost sight of in mathematical expression. Force and energy still look like metaphysical entities.
  2. Psychology is a stumbling block for physics.
  3. To what extent, then, can psychology and physics be separated?
  4. Do the laws of physics become the prime mover of matter?
  5. Is A's physics pre-physics?

## THE PHYSICS

I. An understanding of the central problem should come first. The problem is that of the proper theory or definition of nature. Or we may put the matter this way: in the *Physics,* Aristotle answers the question, What is nature? One may compare the *Psychology:* here he answers the question, What is the soul? This question he answers with two problems in mind, perception and motion. He answers the question about nature with one problem in mind, namely, motion.

II. Nature, about which the question is asked, must first be identified, for the word "nature" is used in several ways, six at least. It had, we may say, both a technical and a literary usage. The technical usage emphasized two things principally: 1) kinds of existence, as when we say that something has the nature of fire, the nature of a plant, etc.; and 2) a kind of motion, as when we say a plant or anything "grows." The literary usage involved a blending of these two, as when we say that man "by nature" or "naturally" desires knowledge, or that "nature does" so-and-so. It involves also collectivity and ellipsis, as, "nature at large" or "as a whole"; and "nature does nothing in vain," meaning that nothing is done in vain. In Aristotle's own usage, the technical and the literary interplay.

III. The confusion consequent to this interplay is relieved by his method of identification. Here, as in the case of the soul, his start is taken, not from definition, but from observation, from an observed distinction, the ordinary distinction between products of nature and products of art, as this distinction is observed in concrete instances of it. Such a concrete instance is found between a plant and a house, a stone and a doorstep. The former is called "nature" or a product of "nature," and the latter "art" or a product of "art." The comparison here with Darwin is suggestive: natural variation and artificial variation. Starting with this observed distinction, Aristotle builds up his theory or definition of nature.

IV. And he builds it up with the problem of motion in

mind. Or we may say that the observed distinction brought the problem of motion to the front. Here Darwin may be compared again: the distinction between natural and artificial variations brought the problem of selection to the front. The procedures of these two men are well worth comparing, especially in view of their effect on the mind. They both go from the obvious to the less obvious. They follow the lead of their subject-matter.

V. What, then, is this observed difference between nature and art? In one respect there seems to be no difference, and in another there seems to be a very important difference.

1. If we disregard the *method* of production, there seems to be no difference. Then everything that is in any sense a product may be called indifferently either nature or art. That is the point of the passage I quoted from the *Physics*. (199a 12)

2. But if the *method* of production is considered, then there is a striking difference. The plant builds itself, but the house does not. In the plant the development or movement from earlier to later is directed from within the plant from the start; in the house this direction is from without.

This distinction, it may be noted, gives us one of the technical uses of the word "nature." It also shows how Aristotle's problem becomes the problem of motion. Nature, as it is now to be examined, is a genetic process; it is a movement from the earlier to the later, from a beginning to an end. It is τὸ τί ἦν εἶναι. This is a very elliptical expression—"The-being-what-was." A plant is "being-what-was-a-seed," a man is "being-what-was-a-child," a doorstep is "being-what-was-a-stone." That is, a plant is what was once a seed, etc. This being now what was once something else is a genetic process, a process of becoming; and this is a movement from a start to a finish.

VI. We may now state the problem of the *Physics;* How are genetic processes to be defined in terms of motion? It is by or through movement that these processes are as an observed fact realized. Hence the problem.

VII. Preparatory to a solution of the problem we have an analysis of the products both of art and nature. As already noted, if the method of production is disregarded, these products are alike or similar. When this likeness or similarity is examined, it is reducible to four characteristics. These are like the four answers we give to the four questions usually asked about any product. These are: 1) What? 2) Out of what? 3) By what? and 4) For what? The answer to the first of these questions identifies the product. The answer to the second exhibits the source from which it comes. The answer to the third exhibits the agency which brought it from that source. The answer to the fourth exhibits the end, purpose, use, or service of the product. Now the Greek verb for question is αἰτεῖν, and the noun for answer or reply is αἴτιον.[1] So Aristotle says that every product involves four αἴτια. This word αἴτιον went into the Latin word *causa* and into our *cause.* So we speak of the four "causes" of Aristotle, and run the great risk of confusion. We might better speak of "factors," since we are dealing with products. Aristotle usually

[1] This etymology is misleading. The sense of αἴτιον as "cause" is derived from αἴτιος, "guilty, responsible for," corresponding to αἰτιᾶσθαι, "complain of, hold responsible." Αἴτιον thus means, as Woodbridge says, the factor responsible for. [C. H. K.]

and at first names the four factors in terms of the four questions, and speaks of *"the* what," *"the* out of which," *"the* by means of," and *"the* for the sake of." This practice, coupled with his use of other terms, led later to speaking of the "formal," the "material," the "efficient," and the "final" cause. Of these the "efficient," being the only one that *does* something, is nearest to our own use of "cause."

Every product is, then, analyzable into four factors, the formal, the material, the efficient, and the final. The analysis, however, does not give these factors as originally independent elements which are somehow combined to produce the product. They are distinguishable but not separable, except as circumstances determine. They make up or are the make-up of the product, but the product is not made up out of them. The product is not an addition of them. They are the distinguishable factors in the genesis of the product. This is important if misunderstanding is to be avoided.

VIII. These four factors, once recognized, are submitted to a further analysis. The formal and efficient together may be set over against the efficient and the final. Form and matter are always together and are correlative. They are also subject to the principle of relativity, and so tend to run out on the one hand to pure form and on the other to pure matter, that is, to form without matter and matter without form. This running out as a consequence of relativity must, however, be kept free from the recognition in nature of either "pure form" or "pure matter." Form and matter are not only inseparable and subject to the principle of relativity, they are also bound up with the genetic process. As this process proceeds, matter exhibits forms it did not exhibit before. We must distinguish between matter with the forms it does have, and with the forms it may or can have, between actual form and potential form. If we ask for the locus of these forms, they are both *in* matter. Plato is criticized on this point. Potential form reduces pure matter to pure potentiality of form.

IX. This distinction between actual and potential forms is important for comprehending the genetic process. Potentiality as such is important. Actuality alone can be an agent or efficient factor. Thus we get out of the analysis of product a preliminary definition of the genetic process: it is a passage or movement from the potential to the actual effected by the actual. The question may now be asked: Which comes first, the potential or the actual? The answer depends on what we mean by "first." They are both "first," but not in the same sense. We may distinguish them as logically first and temporally first, but the clearness of distinction rests on the meaning of the logical and the temporal. It is clear now that there is no temporal relation between the two in the same sense as there are temporal relations of "before" and "after" in the actual.

X. The effective factor is now seen to be always something actual. It may be either external or internal to the product. Note the illustration of a physician curing another and curing himself. This factor is, however, in effect external. The physician who cures himself is not *as physician* also patient.

XI. The final factor may be either internal or external. The end or purpose may be natural or imposed, but no end or purpose can be imposed which matter does not permit. The final and formal factors may consequently merge. The end of a genetic process is final from the point of view of its beginning, formal from its own.

XII. It is now clear that the analysis of the product and the preliminary definition of the genetic process go hand in hand. If we regard the process, form and matter are left as the only relevant factors. This is of great consequence for the logic. The logic is not an independent matter.

The general effect of this analysis of product is to bring the genetic process vividly and concretely before the mind. We now turn to the analysis of motion.

## THE ANALYSIS OF MOTION

I. What is motion? The question is here, first of all, one which asks for identification of subject-matter, or for the usages of a term.

1. From what can be to what is.
2. Getting larger or smaller.
3. Coming to be and passing away.
4. From one place to another.

All these are called "motion." The first is regarded as what natural motion is strictly. The first three may all involve the fourth, but the fourth, although distinguishable from the first, is to be understood in terms of the first. That is, all motion at bottom is a passage from what can be to what is, from potentiality to actuality. The crucial instance here is the so-called transfer of motion through contact.

In the analysis of this instance, Aristotle insists first of all that motion is not separable from body. There is no such thing as motion which operates on bodies to make them move. Bodies *move* or are *in* motion or *at rest*. Consequently each body's motion is its own. Motion is not passed from one body to another, as a man may pass his coat to another man. So in all cases of motion in the fourth sense, bodies are only doing what they can do under the conditions of their doing it. The "transfer" of motion is really the second body's potentiality of motion realized. I shall return to this later. The point here is that the first conception of motion is controlling.

II. Since, however, motion of type 4 is found with the other types, Aristotle examines the accompaniments of this type, namely, infinity, space, time, and void.

III. Infinity. The general notion of "the infinite" is "that which does not give out," that which cannot be exhausted. Belief in the existence of the infinite arises mainly from five considerations:

1. From time—it is infinite.
2. From magnitude—it is infinitely divisible. So the mathematicians hold.
3. From coming to be and passing away: so that nature may not fail.
4. From the limited: it must always be limited by something.
5. Most of all—*thought* never gives out. We can always pass beyond in thought.

   (*a*) There is no absolute or independent infinite. If there were such it would have to be an infinite something; that is, it would have to be distinguishable as a

separate existence from other existences. But such an
existence would be like no other. It would be unintelligible. An infinite something from which all other things
are derived makes the derivation of them unintelligible.
There is no actual infinite.

(*b*) The infinite, however, may be said to exist poten-
tially, but in a special sense; not in the sense that it may
become actual, but in the sense that certain operations
may be endlessly performed. A line is infinite when divided in a certain way; time is infinite; motion; thought;
number is infinite; magnitude is not infinite.

(*c*) Some interesting expressions: "a quantity is infinite,
if it is such that we can always take a part outside what
has already been taken." (207a 8)

"If we take a determinate part of a finite magnitude and
add another part determined by the same ratio, and so on,
we shall not traverse the given magnitude. But if we increase
the ratio of the part, so as always to take in the same amount,
we shall traverse the magnitude, for every finite magnitude
is exhausted by means of any determinate quantity, however
small." (206b 5) "It is not what has nothing outside it that is
infinite, but what always has something outside it." (207a 1)

Nothing numerable can be infinite. "If the numerable can
be numbered, it would be possible to go through the infinite." (204b 8)

The upshot of the analysis is that while it is proper to
speak of infinity, it is improper to speak of "the infinite." We
cannot *start* with the infinite; it is not a principle. The divisibility of a line is not a consequence of its infinity, but its

infinity is a consequence of its divisibility *in a certain way*. In general we have infinity when we have repeatability; and repeatability may have its ground either in nature or in thought. But there is no "infinite" as such. It is improper to say of anything that it is *in* the infinite. In short, "the infinite," if we use the expression, is only the possibility of repetition.[2]

IV. Space. The Oxford translators rarely use the word "space"; they use "place" instead. Their use is justified by the fact that Aristotle apparently never uses τόπος except when boundaries are implied. However, their use is questionable, because it implies to begin with that space is place without boundaries, or place within which all boundaries are contained, or as that within which there are places or positions. These conceptions Aristotle denied *in toto*. He may consequently be said to have denied "space." Even English usage, however, does not restrict space to the Newtonian and Kantian conceptions. We speak of the "space" of this room, and even of a "space" of time. And current ideas about space lead readily to the conception of spaces. Consequently it seems wiser to speak of "space." The Newtonian conception in Greek was probably represented by "the infinite" and "the void," although not wholly so.

That there is space seems evident from the fact of displacement. (208b) Where water was there may later be air and so on, so that the space is different from the water and air. Such conditions may lead us to conclude that there is space apart from body and that every body is in space. But this conclu-

---

[2] See also pp. 57–58, 68.

sion is unsound. Space in concrete instances is a matter of
boundaries, and when there are no boundaries there is no
space. To be in space is to be contained within boundaries.
The idea of a container independent of boundaries is unintelligible. Again: we may speak of the dimensions of space or
directions and distances, so long as we have boundaries to
consider. But without boundaries these dimensions are unintelligible. Suppose there were absolute space, what would it
mean to set up boundaries or dimensions in it? What would
"here" and "there" or "up" and "down" be? What would
"how far" mean?

Given space in the concrete as a matter of boundaries and
dimensions, it is possible to deal with the boundaries and dimensions as the geometers do, but this is not a dealing with
space. Consequently a geometer may prolong a line as far as
he pleases, for what he is then prolonging is the concrete determinate with which he is dealing. He is not drawing an infinite line in an absolute space. The length of his lines and
the size of his figures are of no consequence. A little triangle
is no more and no less a triangle than a big one.

In general then space and bodies go together just as motion
and bodies do. Space has a physical character.

V. The same is true of time. It is in one sense a consequence
of the motion of bodies. These motions are longer and
shorter, faster and slower; they begin and end. The order of
all this is "time." Thus time is also the ordering or measure
or number of motion. For example, when we ask of motion,
how much? we have time as a part of the answer. But absolute time presents the same difficulties as absolute space.

Aristotle's arguments against the independent existence of the infinite, space, time, and void suffer from their dialectical character. For example: to disprove absolute space by argument involves some attempt to deduce consequences from absolute space which are, in fact, invalid. In absolute space there cannot be one "here" distinct from another "here." So the universe cannot be said to occupy any place in absolute space. But what of it? it may be asked. May not absolute space be just what the argument against it makes it out to be? This may be admitted. But the admission makes it clear that absolute space has no determining character whatever. It is not the name of anything identifiable. It does not provide a place where the universe is or can be, for there is no means whatever of defining that place, either theoretically or experimentally. It is wholly lacking in what Aristotle calls actuality. At best it can be only the potentiality of place or position, but when this potentiality is actualized, all places and positions are within the universe.

This seems to be what all the arguments amount to. They convert the supposed absolute into potentialities which when actualized are never actualized in any absolute sense. The actualization is always relative to what is defined to be "within," and never to a distinction between "within" and "without." What is within is obviously never larger or smaller than it is. This means only that largeness and smallness are irrelevant to it as a whole; they are relevant only to its parts in their relation to one another. The sun may be larger than the moon, but the universe cannot be larger than the sun in the same sense. The dimensions of the universe may be, but only on condition that the universe contains the sun. A man's feet may be larger than his hands, but a man is not larger than either of them, for he is not separate from them as they are from each other. In short, the relativity which prevails in the realm of the actual cannot be extended beyond it and remain actual. There can be an empty pitcher but there cannot be an empty universe. Nor can there be an emptiness which comes from outside the universe and fills the pitcher. Nor can there be emptinesses which are moved about within the universe to fill up vacant places.

We must put over against Aristotle's analyses of space, time, etc., his very concrete conception of the world, the universe, the whole or "all." We may say that the world is finite, but with caution. It is not finite as compared with an infinite. It is not set within a frame which contains it, or rather, its frame is not within another frame. It is self-contained. What then is to be said of going beyond thought, and beyond potentiality and actuality?

In sum, there is nothing actual which can be said to be "outside," but only the potential, and when this is actualized it is actualized within. In other words, so far as the universe is concerned, "inside and outside" is "actuality and potentiality." Space, time, and the rest are consequences of the dynamic character of existence, and not the framework of this character.

This seems to be the outcome of Aristotle's argument. The argument is complicated by his insistence on the perceived world. The picture he gives of this world is very concrete. It is a sphere with the earth fixed in the center of it and limited by the sky. In short, it is the earth's spherical horizon—the visible world primarily plus the possibly visible world. Now this much seems clear: we can *think* beyond this world, but we cannot *go* beyond it. Beyond it, there is nothing physical. Thinking beyond it does not carry us physically beyond it. Aristotle is quite explicit on this point. He uses an apt illustration: a man may think beyond his height but that does not make him taller. So we may think beyond the world but that does not make a beyond.

The position may be summed up as follows: the operations in the physical world are all limited by one another. They constitute an interrelated system. By dealing with this interrelated system, thought discovers possible extensions of the various relations involved. These possible extensions, however, are never actual extensions. Whenever they are in any way actualized, they are actualized in terms of the world already existing.

Of this latter he gives an illustration in terms of air and water. When air is changed into water, the bulk of the matter involved shrinks, and when water is changed into air, the bulk stretches, but in both cases all we have is a change from the potential to the actual. What happens is only a redistribution, so to speak, of the relation between the two. There is no total shrinkage or stretching, only an alteration in what can be shrunk and what stretched. Another illustration is growth. In order for a plant to grow, there is not first an empty room ready for it to fill. There is again only an alteration in potentiality and actuality.

It may now be clear what Aristotle is trying to do. He is

trying to substitute for thinking in static categories, thinking in dynamic categories. The ultimate categories are potentiality and actuality; what can be and what is. "The whole," "the all," "the world," etc., can never be reduced wholly to either of them. Now the change from potentiality to actuality is a change in matter. These changes in matter constitute the problem of physics.

The relation between potentiality and actuality should be noted again. No relation which obtains between the actual is here permissible. There is no space-time relation for example. Indeed, the whole trouble, one might say, with physics has been the attempt to construe the relation between the two in terms of the actual. The relation, since it is dynamic, can never be expressed in static terms. However, the fact that the actual is necessary for any release of potentiality, makes a first actual necessary.

This first actual cannot be a first in an endless temporal series.[3] It must be a first in the sense of never having been potential. Thus the crucial problem of the physics is defined.

The problem is not that of creation, for nature presents not a creation but a realization of the potentialities of matter. It is, again, the problem of motion, or we may now say, the problem of how matter is activated.

Another way of statement; infinity, space, time, and void are in one way legitimate and in another way illegitimate. They are legitimate in so far as they arise out of a consideration of bodies and their mutual relations. They are illegitimate when, separated from the consideration of bodies, they

[3] See also pp. 66, 74.

are conceived to constitute a general framework in which the operations of bodies occur. Aristotle consequently denies that they are ἀρχαί in the strict sense. They are not, that is, the beginnings of nature, or that from which nature starts. To make of them the foundation or framework of nature is to court confusion.

The crucial problem of physics is the actualizing of the potentiality of motion. Changes in nature are the change from what can be to what is. Now in the case of bodies A and B, when B moves as a consequence of the impact of A, it is B's motion which illustrates physical change rather than A's, because A is given in motion already; its motion is actual. It is this actual motion of A, or better, it is A in actual motion, coming in contact with B, that releases B's power to move. It is to be noted again that B's motion is not A's motion taken over. We may formulate it that way if we like, but the physical motion is not given in the formula. This point must be kept in mind. (Compare the growth from seed to plant; the plant is the seed's power realized, and not the taking over of the power of sun, air, moisture, etc.) Without A's motion, however, B would not move. So all changes in nature presuppose the actual motion of some body. This body cannot be a first moving body in an endless series. It must be a body always in motion. I do not find it wholly clear just what this body is. At times it seems to be the heavenly bodies themselves in their ceaseless, because circular, movements about the earth or the pole. At times it appears to be the sky as a moving body independent of them, and with a material make-up quite different from them. It is clear, however, that

Aristotle makes all movements under the heavens and sky, or within them, depend for their moving on heavenly movements, or movements in or of the sky. Every motion on the earth or between the earth and the sky is a consequence of motions in the sky, just as B's motion is a consequence of A's. And these motions in the sky are endless, constantly returning on themselves and never ceasing. The physical problem is, thus, apparently solved. The illustration of the sun's going round the earth may serve here again to give a picture of it.

But Aristotle is not content with this solution. Ceaseless and endless actual motions do not satisfy him. The causes of his dissatisfactions are various. (Take up motion before what follows: see paragraph below.) Although natural motion may be reduced for the sake of analysis to the simple type illustrated by A and B, the formal and final factors involved cannot be disregarded. There are in nature movements with specific character, motions which reach ends. This has been exhibited in the case of the soul. Looked at from the point of view of the ends involved, these motions are not only changes from what can be to what is, but they are also realizations more or less complete of characteristic activities. They are motions with a tendency or striving—exhibitions of desire—and they give rise to the good. Their consummation is illuminating. This is particularly true with the soul. The reversal here: the end somehow activating the beginning. Motion is thus awakened desire also.

Ceaseless and endless motion is after all motion. As such it implies ceaseless and endless activation. This activation, however, cannot be conceived simply by repeating the earlier movement. The activation must be of a different sort. There must be an unmoved mover.

## CONCLUDING REMARKS

The *Physics,* the *Metaphysics,* and the *Psychology* of Aristotle should be taken together if one is to have an adequate conception of his theory of nature. The three of them may be read with the first sentence of the *Metaphysics* as a clue to the understanding of them. πάντες ἄνθρωποι τοῦ εἰδέναι ὀρέγονται φύσει. The sentence tempts one to play with it. Ross, in the Oxford English edition, translates it: "All men by nature desire to know." This is good, as good, probably, as one can do. But the Greek has a quality difficult to reproduce in one English sentence. The words of the original and their forms deserve attention. "All men" is simple and clear enough. "By nature" is not so simple. For, as Aristotle says, that word "nature" is used in several senses. It means, for example, that which determines a thing to be what it is and do what it does, as when we speak of the "nature" of fire, and say it is the nature of fire to burn. So we may say that it is the nature of man to know or want to know. As burning is to fire, so is knowing to man. I often think that Spinoza took this first sentence of the *Metaphysics* and turned it into the second axiom of his second book of the *Ethics: Homo cogitat,* man thinks. Thinking or knowing is what man characteristically does; that is his nature. But the word has also

the meaning of a life process, a genetic movement which culminates, so that man thinks or knows "by nature" in the
sense that his life's history is a history in which thinking and
knowing is a genetic process. The seed of the matter is in him,
so to speak, and that seed grows with his growing. So when
we say "by nature," we must keep "nature" dynamic, keep
the suggestion of a life process.

"Desire" is questionable. We might say "desire," implying
some longing or eagerness or wanting. The Greek word has
that flavor, but it has it picturesquely. For the word means
"to stretch out," and particularly to stretch out the hands in
the attitude of asking, supplicating, or demanding, stretching
them out to get something. And as the verb is in the middle
or passive voice, we have: all men by nature stretch out their
hands. And so, if you will, "desire."

It is difficult to improve on "to know." We have an infinitive in the Greek. But we have it with the neuter article,
which transforms a verb into a noun, giving to an action the
sense of a thing done or in the doing. To get this effect in
English we use the participle form of the infinitive as when
we say "running (meaning "to run") is exercise." So "knowing" or "to know" is an exercise. "All men," then, "stretch
out their hands for knowing, or to know or to get that exercise which culminates in knowledge." The desire to know is
not simply a desire for knowledge; it is rather the desire to
exercise the power which ends in knowledge. "Man thinks."

The word "know" should receive attention. Aristotle did
not use it, but he might have used one akin to it, viz.
γιγνώσκειν. This would have been a "practical" word. Com-

pare our "can." He used εἰδέναι. Compare vision. Also εἶδος.[4]

Thus the first sentence of the *Metaphysics* gives us a picture of man in words. We are to see him trying to see, as if he were stretching out his hands for something, reaching out for a light which would make clear. That is what man is like by nature. A proof of this, or a sign of it, says Aristotle, is the delight men have in their senses and especially in the sense of sight. We are thus to see man as a being who wants to see. He sees naturally, for he has eyes, but he wants to see better. He wants to carry his seeing as far as he can or as far as it can be carried. The more care he uses in his seeing, the clearer things and the distinctions between them become, the clearer what he sees becomes. And the more he becomes a theorist or spectator, his seeing becomes "theorizing," but this is only another way of seeing, as the word clearly indicates. So all men by nature want "theory." And to have theory is the consummation of human life. Man does not want to walk in the dark, but in the light. All men by nature reach out their hands for the light which will lighten their going to and fro in the world. Again: man thinks. We must get this picture of man first. In a sense it is the first ἀρχή, start, beginning, principle.

And we must get the picture naively, without distortion and without breaking it up. In all simplicity we must take man looking out upon the world he inhabits, at the earth

---

[4] Aristotle's use of εἰδέναι, "to know," and εἶδος, "form," reflects the importance of vision because both words are derived from the root of ἰδεῖν, "to see." [C. H. K.]

Woodbridge adds in the margin: "The ideate, ideize, to get ideas. Caution here."

and at the sky. For it is the earth and the sky which he
sees, and it is of them he wants the theory. He must never be
allowed to lose sight of his eyes' vision. To be sure, there is
much to be attached, as it were, to what he sees with his eyes
which he does not see with them, sounds, odors, weights,
etc., but his eyes reveal that to which these other things are
attached. Sight is the consummating sense. Without it nothing
would be seen. Those who see may say that those who do not,
grope about in the dark, but strictly they do not *grope*. They
do so only for the seeing. They may be said to touch or hear
or smell, but hardly "about," for "about" is an eye's word.
Thus it is the visible world which is really primary in the
matter of theory. It is the consummation of perception, because whatever other than visible things is perceived, is in the
visible world attached in some way to what is visible.

As I have said, we must take this quite simply and naively.
Here we find nature or the world as the precise and concrete
subject-matter for inquiry. It is what men want to know. It
is what they think about. As this world is examined, man
finds that for the better seeing of it, he must make distinctions
and groupings, such distinctions as space, time, and matter,
quality, quantity, form, subject (or "substance"), accident,
state of being or habitude, what is and what can be, etc., and
such classifications as major and minor, kinds, genera, and
species. All these distinctions and groupings are relevant to
this concrete world and what man says about it. It is their
relevancy to the concrete world that gets expressed in his
language.

In all this clearer seeing of the world, the circumstance of most importance is the distinction between what is and what can be, for it is this distinction which is provoking. When we disregard it, the world is seen to be simply what is. It is like a picture simply looked at with no curiosity about how the picture came to be. One could say a good deal about such a picture, but one would not say much that would be then important. What he might then say gets importance from the neglected distinction. This it is which raises such questions as how? why? what for? Without it, the only pertinent question seems to be, what?

It is in terms of the distinction between what is and what can be that the world is seen to be dynamic, kinetic, genetic, process, development, evolution, the attainment of characteristic ends or finalities. As such it is seen to require motivation. This motivation can be seen up to a certain point, but at that point the question of motivation is not fully answered. It cannot be answered now by continuing the method employed up to that point, for it is characteristic of this method to leave the question without conclusion, however far the method is carried. What then is to be done?

It seems to me that Aristotle here really falls back on his theory of the soul. The source of motivation he is looking for seems to find nowhere else anything like concrete illustration. The sky or the heavenly spheres may demand a kind of motivation different from what they themselves are seen to supply, but they do not directly illustrate or exhibit it. They may demand the divine, but they do not exhibit it beyond that "ever-being" of them which leads men to call them divine. The divine may move them, but they afford no clue.

Now man with his soul illustrates the natural dynamic or genetic process. And he is clearly the best illustration of it, because of the fact that in him this process is carried to that consummation where the desire for theory is actualized in definite concrete form. Here attained vision is found to be the discovery of the light by which he walks and lives. Here are discovered the conditions of change and movements. Here is developed the logical framework, which to be sure does nothing, but is nonetheless that without which nothing could be done. Here are found the conditions without which what can be could never become what is. These conditions are not material conditions, they are not bodies of matter. They are not grasped with the hand or seen with the eye. They are things of the mind, as we say. They are logical because they are what is finally said by man in his theory. And they have the effect of releasing power as nothing else releases it. They do not push and pull a man about, but when once they are there, in his mind, all his being pushed and pulled is seen to be in consequence of them. They are in him an unmoved mover. They are "the divine" in him, the kind of motivation which nature ultimately demands. For it is a logic of its occurrences that is demanded.

So it is at last the logical that moves the world. The divine is the logical or what the logical expresses. It is a life, because the logical with man is a life, the life of reason. So the divine life is the life of thought, but of thought independent of that material approach to it which marks the growth of man's soul. It is νόησις νοήσεως. His life is always like ours when at its best.

Aristotle calls God very concretely a living being. He is, however, obviously not picturable. He is reached not by the imagination, but by thought. Spinoza should be compared here. God is that without which nothing can be or be conceived, but with which everything that is or is conceived has its actuality.

Why then, given God, does not everything happen? Matter and chance no less than God are factors in the cosmos.

Aristotle's theory of nature is on its negative side a protest against his predecessors. Against Democritus and Empedocles he protests that nature cannot be understood as a rearrangement of elements which are themselves inert and changeless. Such a view has these consequences:

1. It neglects the facts of growth and qualitative change.

2. It requires that power, ability, energy, force be always actual as matter is.

3. It converts perception, thought, and motion into a rearrangement of elements and so leaves the passage from one rearrangement to another without any motivation.

Against Plato he protests that the separation of forms from matter is not justified either by observation or reasoning. The locus of forms is always matter.

On the positive side, he attempts a dynamic theory of nature, and looks at nature as the realization of possibilities. In working this out he also is driven at last to the question of motivation. His answer is that motivation is ultimately logical. This is difficult. He finds support for his view in:

1. The effect of the possession of knowledge. Knowledge shows that there is a formula for whatever occurs. What can

be may never become what is, but there is always a rule for
its becoming. Both the intelligibility of the process and the
control of it by art involve this rule. Without this rule it seems
impossible that the change could occur, and the rule seems to
be independent of the occurring. The rule is always and the
occurrence now and then. Given the rule, the change will
occur, unless it is hindered. It is matter and chance that hin-
der. His psychology helped him here because: (*a*) it did not
separate soul and body; (*b*) it insisted that reason is not an
outgrowth of perception but an exercise or life beyond bodily
limitations.

2. His analysis of motion. Motion always involves the actualizing of the ability or power to move. Bodies are not only
affected but they realize their powers. There is always a direction of these powers. This direction realized is the fulfillment of the bodies' powers. Motion is thus a means of
attaining what is desired, but what is desired ultimately is
knowledge.

Booth Tarkington once said: Man could always have flown
but he did not know how. [5] Given, then, a world in which
flight is possible if the conditions of it are known, it looks as
if man would one day fly.

This ultimate insistence on the logical Aristotle converts
into a theology. That is, he makes the recognition of the
ultimately logical, the recognition of that sort of reality which
men assign to gods. It is the ever-living, or ever-being source
of the order and government of nature. It is not the creator
or source of the world, but only of its order and government.

[5] Booth Tarkington, *The Spider,* a short story.

We might then call this God the principle of order and government.

Aristotle is illustrative of all theorists of nature, all cosmologists.

1. The evident fact of process, change, development, evolution, history. Starting and stopping.

2. The incompleteness of cosmology when it attempts to make the process of starting and stopping complete and self-contained. The completion always in terms of the ever-being or ever-living.